LOST FATHER

AN INSPIRATIONAL FICTION NOVEL
PATH TO FAMILY BOOK 1

WRITTEN BY
LEIGH LINCOLN

ISBN: 978-1-960136-51-0

Table of Contents

CHAPTER 1

Colorado – Present Day

"Hey, you going to drink that? Or are you going to continue hugging that beer mug like it's your new best friend?" A voice broke the quiet stillness that had enveloped me since I'd been handed my libation. Not a particularly deep one, but it sounded a bit on the raspy side. Either he hadn't slept in a while or he smoked.

Not like I cared one way or the other.

As my mind raced to form some type of response, I reflected on how swiftly my life had changed—on how my whole life had turned upside down in the blink of an eye. With no warning, no way to know what lay around the corner. Yesterday, life had been normal, safe, secure. Everything had followed the same pattern and routine as always. We're old, my wife, Nancy, and I; not much of life left to live anymore. No room for anything special to happen. And this was my first mistake—thinking that when you hit a certain age you become immune to problems.

I debated whether I should ignore this interruption into my deep funk; just continue to sit here and wallow in my pity party of one. Or if I should dig deep and find some half-assed answer to give. One that would shut down any and all future questions from the jokester behind the bar.

In the end, I squinted up at the man who'd dared to intrude on my dark musings. I hadn't given him more than a passing glance when I'd planted myself on this rock-hard, unsteady stool. Heck, I hadn't taken in the room when I'd entered beyond the fact the bar remained empty on this cold, wet, dreary afternoon. To be honest, both the weather and the silence suited my current mood perfectly.

No, after hauling my sorry ass inside I'd managed to do almost nothing. What with my heart having been torn out as it had, my soul left in shreds. Leaning my elbows on the edge of the rough wood, I rested my head on my hands. Squeaking out a simple request for a cold one, I stared with blank eyes at the wavy grain embedded in the wood. This dark counter I'd happened to find myself propped against remained sturdy under me. Solid enough to hold me up since I'd become incapable of doing that on my own.

Didn't matter the brand of beer the man might hand me. Didn't matter if the beverage was ice cold or tepid. The only important thing had been to make sure I paid the price of admission. I hadn't wanted to end up getting the bum's rush and thus be forced to drive somewhere else. My body couldn't handle that in its current state. Do believe even moving to a different seat in this bar might have been beyond me at that particular juncture. My very bones had melted inside me, leaving me a puddle of mush.

The person standing before me wasn't what I expected. The

bartender appeared to be in his late twenties or early thirties. His face sported the scruff of a beard not quite shaved but not quite grown in, either. The vibe his disheveled sandy blonde hair gave off matched his not-quite-clean half-apron. The formerly white linen now dull, spotted with grease, grime, and goodness knew what, the strings of which he'd tied at his right hip in a loose knot rather than a bow.

Rather obvious the man didn't care one iota how he looked. Not to mention the fact he wore a bright orange T-shirt with a bleach spot shaped like the face of a lion on one shoulder. And as if to add further abuse to those who might look his way, the front of it bore an insult. Yep, a large green neon hand gave the middle finger to the world and shone bright in the middle of his shirt. Not sure if that was the best thing for someone in the hospitality industry to be wearing. But right at this moment I sure wished I had one to wear as well. I wanted to tell everyone and their mother to take a flying leap into nowhere and leave me the frick alone. I didn't want to explain myself, or my rather poor choices in my very long, irresponsible life, to anyone.

However, given what had happened this morning, today, or at the very least, someday very soon, I'd have to. In the meantime, I'd found myself somewhere I shouldn't have been. Once again I'd found myself being my true self, the reckless, do-whatever-the-heck-I-want-to self. And right at this second, what I wanted to do was get plastered. I'm a man who tends to have one drink, then another, and then never stops. And drinking was yet another of those oh-so-many things I shouldn't be doing.

Hey, it's five o'clock somewhere, right?

Giving a quick scan of the place, I realized how old, dingy, dim, and decayed the room around me appeared to be. And not because the weather had painted the whole world a dark shade of grey—despite the fact that my watch face told me the time was about noon, the sun remained hidden from view. In this room, half the lightbulbs were burned out. I doubted the joint had been given a proper scrubbing in years. Tables leaned to one side or the other. Chairs had strings tied beneath them to keep the legs together. Molting heads of dead animals hung in various spots on the walls. Deer, bear, moose, bison, a few smaller things as well. Their glassy eyes stared at me, shaming me from wherever it is animals go when they die. Numerous neon signs for beer and liquor companies also adorned the joint. None of them were fully lit, thus 'beer' was now 'bee' or 'be r' on most of them. Others were blinking in a weird pattern that their makers never intended.

I tapped the side of my mug with a ragged fingernail, the glass no longer cold, the rich foam long gone. Pondering if I should take another sip, or if I'd even had one from the beer at all. I decided against taking even a drop of the brew, knowing the path it'd lead to. Yet, today, my mouth watered for this beer. No, I needed something stronger. Something to take the edge off, to ease my tattered nerves.

Taking another look around, I wondered if I'd managed to somehow do the impossible. If somehow I'd stepped into a wormhole, ending up in a parallel universe. Everything around me gave off the vibe of another time, another place. Everything a wee bit off and wrong somehow.

But no, my luck wasn't good enough to have ended up in some weird sci-fi movie. My reality is my reality. I'd done what I'd done. And I'd ended up here of all places in the world I might have chosen to escape to. I'd have to admit this was a far sight better than the last hellhole I'd landed in when I'd taken off. All because I hadn't wanted to face my problems. Okay, problem. No, not a problem. A baby. A blessing I should've accepted for everything it was worth when I'd been given it.

His shoulders gave a slight shrug, "Rough day? Or just the weather making you a bit out of sorts?" He gave a half-hearted swipe at the sticky counter with a greyish-looking rag he pulled from his back pocket. He didn't seem to mind that I hadn't opened my mouth to answer his first set of ridiculous questions.

"Look, I didn't come in here to yammer with someone. Men don't spill their guts. They have a beer and deal with it, okay?!" I slapped my right hand on the counter.

The force rattled my full-to-the-brim mug enough that liquid sloshed over the side, splashing my arm. I glanced down at the dots of the brownish slush as they dripped off my blue flannel shirt onto the wood. The resulting squiggles danced along an almost unseen seam in the close-knit boards. Flowing together toward nowhere. My life in a nutshell.

As I shifted my gaze back toward my unwanted companion, he didn't appear phased at all by my outburst. Instead, his eyes were now opened wide, his lips turned up into a hint of a smile. Nope, he looked more like a cat about to catch his mouse.

"Ah, you're exactly like my dad used to be. Old school man's man. Can't let a pesky little thing like feelings get in the way of life, huh?" He gave a small chuckle as he shook his head. "Well, let me tell you what that got him. An early grave. Yup, he had a heart attack right here behind this very bar." He patted the edge of the counter.

"He bottled up his emotions until he exploded one night while pulling a draft. Not like any of the guys in here cared much from what

I heard about the event later. They just screamed about not getting their beers in a timely fashion. Never mind, not important. But it's why I'm here, right now, with you. Enjoying this lovely day, in this super awesome spot. I inherited this place years ago. Even now, I still can't decide if I should stay or sell it. And as you can see," he waved his hand around the room, sweeping over the whole area.

The dingy rag dangled from his slim fingertips, showing off a perfect manicure. "I don't care nor know very much about running a bar. Good thing you ordered a draft, who knows what you'd have gotten if you'd asked for some fancy cocktail!"

With that, I took a deep chug of the lukewarm beer, trying to dodge having to give any kind of response. The drink hit me like a brick, causing my swirling stomach to revolt. Swiping my mouth with the back of my hand afterward, I managed to hide the fact I needed to belch in the worst way. Instead, I let out a tiny 'urp' and released some of the pressure building up inside of me.

Sentiments, feelings, and memories from years ago now forced their way to the surface. All of which dared me to no longer ignore them, to face them head-on. Was any of what he said true? Did stuffing all of those things away cause heart or health problems? Naw. My not-so-great health came from being older than dirt. Not from pretending to be someone I wasn't for the better part of fifty years.

Even so, I gave my new mate another good long look. Today, of all days, I do believe I needed someone like him. Someone who was a straight shooter. No holds barred, give me the punch in the face I deserved. Even if it was only in the metaphorical sense. After all, that's what had turned my life in the right direction once before. Someone being so direct I had no choice but to fly straight.

Until now.

This morning had started like every day had for years. Nancy made our simple meal of toast, fruit, and coffee. No butter for that toast, no jam either. No creamer or sugar for the coffee either, milk alone. Long gone are the days when bacon and eggs were on the menu. No, some stupid doctor at some point had nixed almost everything that had any flavor in it. All because of cholesterol or high blood pressure or some other nonsense.

I'd managed to choke down the meal in silence, and she'd never stopped blabbing about this or that. I'm deaf to whatever vile things she has to say by now. I don't care who's sleeping with whom. I don't care who had a car accident. I don't care who got drunk at the local brewery. I don't care whose grandchild is pregnant out of wedlock. I don't care about any of it and haven't for a rather long time.

After our sparse meal, she wandered out of our tiny apartment to go on her daily walk with the other bitties. We live in a wonderful retirement community, filled with others also one step away from death. I sank down onto the couch. Well, more like a loveseat since the thing only has the space to seat about two and a half people. It's this hideous purple color, Nancy loves it because it's the same color as the drapes. To me, it looks for all the world like a lilac threw up.

For about half a second, I debated flipping on the TV or grabbing the computer which lives on the side table. That little table doubles as the sole bookshelf as well; I'd added a few boards under the top to make this happen. Once again, I sat here missing our old house where I had the space for an office. A place of retreat for moments of quiet and stillness.

That wasn't possible in this cramped apartment with its efficient layout. We had a kitchen/breakfast nook with a postage-stamp-sized patio beyond the sliding door; a living room big enough for only the tiny couch and a TV hanging on the wall; a bathroom with a shower, no tub, same as a travel trailer; and the lone bedroom, large enough for our double bed, dresser, and a single nightstand.

The entire space we now called home would fit in the living room of our former house. The idea constantly depressed me as the walls hemmed me in, making me believe I lived in a cage or a prison.

In the end, I opted for silence, a few moments of peace after the barrage from Nancy at breakfast. Reaching over, I slid the computer onto my lap. Opening its clamshell lid, I pulled up the browser. Wondering for a second if I should read the news, maybe a few emails or do whatever else online. Never expecting anything unusual to happen. Because nothing out of the ordinary ever did. I'm old, stuck in a very deep rut, boring myself to death. Which would be any day now if I could only be so lucky.

But today didn't turn out to be like every other day for the last twenty- or thirty-something years. Since my mood already skewed low, reading the news didn't appeal to me. Who needed to hear about the latest shooting? The newest dumb move Congress or the current crackpot president had made? What this stupid celebrity had said? Nope, not for me today. Nancy would fill me in on all the details later after she watched the talk shows and scanned social media.

I decided to check my email and I spotted a rather odd subject line: 'THIS ISN'T SPAM, I know you don't know me…' Curiosity got the better of me and I opened the message.

Huge mistake.

No, I made my mistake years and years ago. This was my reckoning.

Staring at the words on the screen, they fluttered in and out of focus. Removing my glasses, wiping them on my soft undershirt, and replacing them on my nose didn't help matters. My breath started to come in pants, faster and faster. My hands clenched into fists; I squeezed them tighter and tighter. I wanted to scream, punch something, cry, oh, I didn't know what.

With no warning, a calm washed over me. Then a wave of fear— was this a scam? No; I scanned the top part of the email again. Tucked into this were too many details only she might know. Things I'd never shared with anyone. Specific little facts that a select few were aware of but hadn't seen the light of day in over fifty years.

My stomach lurched; the truth lay in these words. It hadn't been buried and forgotten, though to be honest, this had to be expected. A thing like this couldn't be wished away, no matter how hard you tried.

I slammed the computer shut, not caring if I cracked the screen. Throwing it to the far corner of the couch, I rose. I stomped around our apartment for a minute, going first into the hall, then to the kitchen, then back to the living room again. The walls started to press in on me, this space far too small for pacing. Given what I'd just read, even the national forest we lived near wouldn't be a large enough place for me to get my feelings out.

Sweat poured out of every inch of me despite the cool of the morning. The faint breeze from the patio door that Nancy had left ajar brushed against my face; I shifted a bit to be closer. This resulted in my skin becoming clammy and uncomfortable, and I moved away one step. And I began to shuffle around our space once again.

Stopping, I stood in the center of our tiny home, just behind the couch and right next to the dining table in the nook. From here it's possible to spot almost every inch of our apartment.

I paused to take note of each and every feature our lives had boiled down to. The lone photo from our unusual wedding, snapped right as we kissed. A few photos of Lisa taken over the years—baby, teen, young woman, young mom, middle-aged career woman. A few trinkets Nancy and I had picked up along our journey together—knickknacks from the old farmers' market, things I'd carved when I worked at various campgrounds, the paintings she'd made of waterfalls and animals.

I was about to blow this world of ours to smithereens. Because of something I did in another life. Before I'd met Nancy. Before a lot of things.

I stormed outside and jumped into our old powder blue Ford sedan without leaving a note for my wife. I didn't have any idea how to let her know what was going on. I didn't even give her a glance as I flew by their tight-knit group walking along the road near the entrance to the complex. Because she knows nothing about the matter—well, almost nothing. And I needed to keep it that way for as long as possible. Because, right at this moment, I had no words to say.

Not thinking about much of anything, a sole idea came to me—I needed to run. Again. Once in the car, other thoughts started to rush through my mind. Each one crashed like waves against the wall I'd built around memories from my former life. Destroying my defenses, letting everything come to the surface.

All the lies. Years and years of telling my wife she was the only one, that I'd never been with a girl before her. However, not only was she not my first, but I'd known all along a child might be out in the world somewhere.

And now I struggled to grasp the certainty of this. She had a name—Jenny. I muttered the name one too many times as the first few miles flew by, then did my best to shut all thoughts of her out of my head and heart. Just as I had tried to do all those years ago, when this child had been nothing more than an illusion. An image I'd conjure up, picturing the child's mother more than the child itself.

About a hundred miles later, my legs cramped something fierce from my pent-up tension. No, not from driving in the pouring rain for over an hour. A late fall storm had sprung up despite almost no clouds having been in the sky. Soon after I'd taken flight the heavens had opened wide and released all of their fury. A squall so fierce that spotting the car in front of me became almost impossible even with my wipers on high.

Nor was my problem the traffic which had been unusually heavy given the weather. Where everyone else might be heading on such a disaster of a day wasn't a concern of mine. Yet the bumper-to-bumper cars on the freeway left me screaming in frustration by the end of my journey. And though my words were about the situation around me, my thoughts weren't on those other idiot drivers. I supposed my shouting, "Move it, you stupid piece of…" was a form of distraction to keep my mind from thinking about that email.

Even so, my defense wore down. Somewhere around mile seventy-five, her words kept popping into my mind: "I'm your daughter." Stuck on repeat, an endless loop.

After realizing the impossibility of driving further, I took the next exit I happened upon. I fled the muddle the freeway had become. The water on the roadway into the town splashed around my car, everywhere around me a soggy mess. Beside the road, a river now pooled and ran down the ditch in a swift whirl of brown muck filled with debris and twigs. The town at the end of the road didn't matter.

The bar I happened to find at the edge of that town also didn't matter. No, the important thing here was ignoring the bomb that had been hurled into my life mere moments ago. No, Jenny couldn't and shouldn't be called something destructive like a bomb. That's not fair of me. She's flesh and blood. Someone I'd helped create a lifetime ago.

And now here I sat a heartbeat later, trying to figure out what to say to a stranger. Or if, in fact, I should say anything at all. Would it be easier to speak my truth to someone I didn't know?

Unlikely.

"This situation is a bit more complicated than me not wanting to get all touchy-feely, young man." Pausing for a moment, I raked a hand through my thinning, white hair as I raised my head a fraction. All to end up staring deep into the eyes of a tan rabbit mounted on a plank fixed on the wall. I shivered as an eerie feeling of dread crept over me.

What if I had become as hollow as these stuffed animals?

I reflected on the fact that in a few more years this whole thing wouldn't matter. I'd be senile or dead. Why had she contacted me now? After all this time? Fine, the answer to that question had been in the email. DNA. She'd taken a test, found a common link, and that had led her to me. No getting around something as fundamental as that. Technology not only made my life harder on a daily basis but had now caused my past to catch up with me. The noise of shuffling feet caused me to shift my gaze back toward my host.

I watched as he turned a bit, grabbing two new glasses from the massive, glass-door fridge behind him. He drew a beer from the tap, sliding it towards me before removing my first, almost untouched one. Pulling another beer, he gulped half of it, refilling it before placing it on the counter before him.

"Well, as you can see, I've got nothing better to do than have a beer with a friend. You're the first customer I've had all week." He reached out his hand, "Hi, my name's Ryan. Nice to meet you."

I hesitated; I hadn't been looking for a friend or a confessor when I walked into this hole-in-the-wall bar, what, an hour ago? More? Not like it mattered how long I'd been slumped on this stool. But to refuse his gesture would be tantamount to a slap in the face. He was doing his level best to make me feel welcome, comfortable. Anything he could do to give me the space to work out whatever problem had led me in here.

Why is it that so many bartenders think they can be shrinks? My best guess is because so many TV shows and movies have a friendly bartender. One who fixes everyone. Yup, give them half an hour or an hour, and, poof, every issue, no matter how great, is solved. And of course, this is done by none other than your friendly, neighborhood barkeep.

But life ain't that simple.

"I'm Bruce." I grabbed his offered hand in a meaty, powerful grip. Unlike my hand, which is rough, callused, and worn, his hand was soft, baby smooth. He winced; I released the pressure and grabbed my glass instead.

I gave a loud sigh; might as well talk to someone. I couldn't tell any of this to my wife, that's for darn sure. Not yet at least. I'd bet my life I'd have to at some point. Nancy deserved to hear the truth and that information should come from me. Not from some random stranger. Okay, my child wasn't exactly random. Nor was she exactly a stranger. Just someone I hadn't met yet.

Still, I needed to get a handle on what those words in that darn email meant before I said anything to Nancy.

On some level, for years I'd known I'd have to face everything somewhere along life's journey. Face him or her. My heart gave a squeeze, my breathing stopped, pain filled me. Until today, I hadn't even known the sex of the child, my child.

How had I been such a coward? How had I never once even asked a few simple questions? Why did I never go back and act like a damn man? Stand up, admit that this is what I did, that I'm ready to deal with whatever consequences may come my way.

Easy—I didn't want to face the memories of Nam again. Nor did I want to risk seeing Donna ever again. But at the very least I should've called.

But where? And whom? Did she stay in my hometown? Did she go back to hers? I shook my head, so many things I'd never wanted to think about. So many things I'd chosen to forget. So much simpler to pretend my life began the day I'd arrived in Colorado.

"I got a girl pregnant my freshman year in college. Until today, I didn't know she had the baby." Lamest excuse ever, of course a baby had been born at some point.

I sighed. "Well, I mean, a lot of things might have happened after she'd told me about her, uhm, condition." My head dropped to my chest, my words sounding far off to my ears. Almost as if someone other than me had spoken them. Coming back to me as nothing more than a whisper. I'd never told anyone this. Ever. Only Donna and I were aware of the pregnancy.

Scratch that, Donna might have told everyone in the whole wide world after I fled the scene.

"Ah, now that's not so complicated. Did your girl raise it? Or give it up?" I looked up a bit as he took a more tempered sip of his drink. He proceeded to wipe the foam off his beard and mustache with the tip of a thin finger.

How could he make light of something I'd been wrestling with off and on for over fifty years? Yes, I'd gotten married later and had another child. Yet, so often I'd watch my daughter, Lisa, and have waves of guilt over a child I couldn't even be sure existed. When she took her first steps. When she started kindergarten. When she got the solo in the band concert in eighth grade. When she graduated from college. When she got married. When she presented me with my first grandchild.

But was that even my first grandchild? Was another one out there in the universe? A part of me who didn't even know I existed any more than I was aware of him or her? A better word for this mess was confused rather than complicated.

I raised my head to stare straight into the eyes of the young man before me. Did he look a bit like me? Did he look even faintly like Donna? How many others had I come across over the years and wondered the exact same thing?

And so much guilt ate at me because I had left and had no idea what might have happened afterward. And now my child had emailed me out of the blue. Today. I'd been eating breakfast and she'd been writing that missive. Had she wrestled over the right words to say? Or had she rushed through them, filled with excitement to finally find what she'd been searching for?

I hadn't a clue what to do, how to respond, how to react in response. Somewhere out in the universe, Jenny waited for a reply— from me. From this person she now had come to view as her true father. She needed and deserved answers to her questions. And I'm sure she had a million of them. All of which I would never be able to answer to either of our satisfaction.

But most of all, my gut screamed at me that she would be angry. That she hated me. For leaving her. For never coming back. For not seeming to have ever given a damn about her. Because all she had known would be the world where she'd been abandoned by both her birth parents.

"My daughter was given up for adoption." I swallowed hard, the pain of a rock tearing down my throat as I did. Time to rip the band-aid off, show the world what kind of monster I am at my very core.

"When Donna told me about her pregnancy, I told her it was her problem. As in, not mine, she should deal with it on her own. The next day, I went and enlisted. Headed off to Vietnam shortly afterward. Never looked back. Never even returned to my hometown, not once after that, which is saying a lot. Family was everything when I was growing up, I even went to the local college in my hometown. That's the college we met at, the college I left with no notice. I disappeared, leaving everyone and everything behind without saying a word."

"Dude, while I get you might not have wanted a kid when you were in college…" He gave a slight cough, "Uhm, uncool."

"To say the least." I attempted to take a drink, more to have something to do with my shaking hands than for anything else. But the liquid started to dribble down my chin due to the unsteadiness of my grip. Placing the glass back on the counter, I almost tipped it over. Clutching the handle tight to keep the thing upright, I grimaced. "I'm one of the world's biggest cowards."

I swiped most of the mess off my face, but it didn't and couldn't remove the stain of my sin from my life.

"No way man, you went off to fight in a war. That must count for something!" He swiveled a bit, pointing to a picture hung on the wall behind the cash register.

One of those shots that almost every military guy seems to send home. A huddle of men posing in green T-shirts, camo pants. Half-smoked cigarettes hanging out of their mouths, laughing at the camera, a Jeep in the background.

"My dad in all of his glory, Gulf, yah know." Ryan's face lit up with pride, eyes wide, grinning from ear to ear.

I stared at the yellowing photo for a moment. Wondering what my mother had thought for years when I never came home. I'd sent one simple, quick note from California that I'd arrived back in the States. The day I'd bought my truck, the day I'd decided to go AWOL.

But my mother alone remained the main string tying all of my past together. A connection to the life on the farm I hadn't wanted. To the girl I'd tossed aside, and to a baby that may exist but I didn't want to care about at all. And most of all, my mother had full knowledge of where I'd been the previous few months. In my mind, in order to start from scratch nothing from that life could remain. So I never contacted her again.

Up and landed in another state, where I proceeded to make up a whole story of who I was and where I was from. The word Texas never crossed my lips. I'd never even had a girlfriend before Nancy. I'd never been to college, probably never even mentioned finishing high school. And I for damn sure never went to Nam. Because before the wonderful world of the internet, reinventing yourself was simple.

Nothing more than a matter of telling people what you wanted them to believe. No proof needed, a man's word was his bond. No questions were ever asked. Turned out to be rather easy to start from scratch; I'd never had a social security number before Colorado. I'd been born at home, worked on the family farm, gone to a community college. No paper trail except a military one existed. And I never admitted being in the service to anyone. The day I walked into the office in Colorado to get a driver's license, all I had to say was my parents' names and my birthday. And I didn't even give the real names of my parents. Easy as pie.

Thus, my wife ended up being told lie upon lie. But the biggest one of all remained the one I regretted the most. I boldly made the claim that both my parents were dead, not just the one. In the end, I robbed my daughter of the opportunity to have her grandmother in her life.

So many things were wrapped up in the whole situation. I tried with everything within me to become the man I wanted to be and ended up being one I shouldn't have been. A cheat, a liar, a coward, dishonest to the core. I didn't see a good way to explain any of this to anyone. I flat out shouldn't have ever done what I did.

I groaned, long and deep. One thing alone remained in this giant jumble I'd created out of my life that might be possible to set straight. Well, that and the mess I'd created of so many other lives. I was no hero.

"My service didn't count for anything. Not really. I never saw action. Glorified servant, nothing more. In country for less than two months. The day I got to Colorado, I started dating another girl. We got married a couple of months later. Had a kid right after that. So, I've got two daughters who are about a year apart."

I rapped on the dark wood with my knuckles, my mind going back again to those years. So much more was involved in my war experience than the simple words I'd said. Things left behind in the rubble, things left undone, things best left in the past.

The look on Ryan's face was a mix of puzzlement, pain, and

something I couldn't quite put my finger on. He twisted his lips as he tilted his head, debating what to say next. "Okay, but something happened to change you. Right? You came back from Nam different, you jumped into marriage right away, into fatherhood as well. What gave you that kick in the rear?" His head tipped a bit as he nodded toward my mangled hand. "Was it that?"

I slid my hand off the counter, down onto my lap. Another lie, no one had been told how I'd been injured. But right now, I didn't feel the need to be dishonest. Yet, he didn't need to know that part of the story quite yet. "No. Death." No way around that either. I may not have been assigned to the front lines but in war, the grim reaper still has a way of finding you. "I had love and gave it up out of fear. All to face the worst humanity has to offer."

"So, you loved your gal?" He squinted at me, "But you still left, no word, no goodbye?"

"Even now, I think Donna may have been the best thing that ever happened to me. She changed the way I looked at myself and the world around me." An image floated into my mind, one I hadn't seen in a very long time.

"Hey, we're all young and dumb once." He grimaced. "Okay, I'm still dumb, and I'm not so young anymore. Yet, I don't think I can say I've found 'the one.' That perfect girl who can make me be a better man. Can you say that about this Donna?"

"In the end, I guess not. But because of her, my life changed forever. Which in some ways may be the same thing." I swiped my hand over my face before taking another long drink of my beer. "No, that's unfair. Donna might have been perfect, but I was always flawed. It wasn't possible to make me a better man."

CHAPTER 2

Texas – 1967

For me, college had become a not-to-be-missed milestone in my young adult life. Being the first one in my family to attend, I carried the weight of everyone on my back. Mother, aunts, uncles, cousins. They all had scrimped and saved to make this happen for me. Which was why the family farm no longer remained in my mother's name. Yes, the deed to the simple farmhouse she'd lived in most of her adult life still bore her name. But the bulk of the land had been swallowed up by the larger farm my uncle owned next door.

Yet in the times we lived, something more important than education lurked in the shadows. And this soon became the driving force behind this desire for me to attend. Not for me, but for my mother. She insisted that being in school would keep me safe from the draft. Based on what everyone had learned by then, maintaining good grades almost always earned one a waver. This is if, heaven forbid, their number got called. Thus, no dreading the draft lottery for me, Vietnam wouldn't be in my future. Not now, God willing, not ever.

My uncle, a WWII veteran, who often would regale us kids with war stories, didn't believe my mother should discuss the evils of the current war. To him, military service was sacred, no matter the politics behind the event. Being a boy, I loved the tales of comradery, standing up for our country, defeating our foes.

At the family dinner my mother would often ramble on, "Did you hear 'bout the Henderson boy? He left for Nam a few months back? Well, his momma told me he's coming home. Not sure when. But he's in a hospital somewhere. That ain't gonna be you, Bruce. I'll drag you off to class and take your tests myself if'n I has to."

I'd nod as I shoveled in more mashed potatoes and gravy.

"Now, Helen, don't scare the boy." My uncle would tap his fork on the table, staring at his sister.

Or my mother would state, "Did you hear 'bout the Wilson girl? She's goin' to stay the summer with her aunt, might not come back at all. And that's why, I'm always telling you to keep your hands off girls, Bruce. You get some poor girl in trouble and we ain't shipping her off. No siree, I'd make you live with the shame. Best not do nuttin' in the first place. You hear me? Because somethin' like that might get you kicked out of college. And then where's you gonna be?"

I'd nod and continue to gnaw on my gristly piece of steak.

"Goodness, Helen, hush your mouth!" My uncle would slam down his beer bottle and glare at her.

Nothing for me to do in the face of this.

My mother always had a story, a way to make me feel guilty for something I had no intention of doing. So, no, my mother's precious baby boy, only child, main provider for her future needs couldn't go off and fight in some war.

Not like she didn't bleed red, white, and blue as a good American patriot should. Every 4th of July she'd be at the picnic with every other woman in town with her best pie for the annual town bake-off. She'd wave an American flag during every parade our town ever had. Put her hand on her heart and sing along with the national anthem every time it was played—at games, at the school, whenever. Plus, she'd cried for days after Kennedy had been shot. Her heart and loyalty belonged to Uncle Sam—after God, Jesus, and the Holy Ghost, that is.

However, to display her American pride by sending me off to some God-forsaken place to play soldier remained off the table. No way, no how would she allow that. Some sacrifices were too great to contemplate. Even the loss of one of my fingers in the service of our country was asking for more than she was willing to give. Other families had children. As in plural. It would be possible for them to lose one and he wouldn't be missed as much. Whereas I was irreplaceable because I was one of a kind.

Irrational thinking on her part, I'm well aware. All children are dear to their mothers, loved to pieces, and grieved when they come home in a box.

The reasoning behind her fears had a rather simple explanation. My father had passed after several months of agonizing torture. Injuries he'd sustained in a farming accident, dying in their shared bed inch by inch. I don't remember much about that; I was five at the time. My mother relied heavily on family, community support, and faith at the time.

About the age of ten, I began to toil on the family farm alongside my million and one cousins. However, being the eldest, I held a certain status in the family they would never achieve. When they reached the age of ten, most of them stopped their lessons and just worked on the farm. I often heard grunts of disgust when I drew near. They knew same as I did, their labors benefited me more than themselves. While I had my chores in the early morning, and a few upon returning from school, after dinner I was free to focus on learning.

Thus, I went to school every day it was in session, listening with great intent to each lesson. I completed my homework each night, no matter how late that required me to be up because I wasn't the sharpest tool in the shed. Still, my mother wanted something more for me than being a poor dirt farmer in West Texas. Therefore, I studied with all my might to achieve her goals.

What I wanted didn't seem to matter to anyone.

Yet, a tiny part of me found I enjoyed learning. Up to a point, that is. When the local veterinarian came to help with a cow having a breach birth or a horse coming up lame, I'd rush to his side. I'd hammer him with question after question about what he was doing. If I had to go to college, might as well find something interesting to study while I was there. And healing an animal felt right to me.

Something else lay hidden in the shadows. My mother's fragile strength keeping things together had suffered far more than it should. And it wasn't going to be enough to hold up under the stress of another great loss. Her grief over the death of my father never quite ended. Too many nights I'd hear weeping escaping from behind the closed door of her bedroom. While we never discussed her bouts of sadness, it hung heavy in the air.

As I grew, a small part of me was aware I should never dare to break her heart as my father had. Because it might very well be the death of her.

Yet, all of my mother's plans for my life came to dust. Within a few days of starting classes my freshman year of college, my sense of self began to shift. I began to form into a man even I didn't quite recognize.

All because I started listening to my new friends. Young men who hadn't lived in the back of beyond Texas all their lives. Guys who I believed had a good bit more insight about the world than I did. And I began to desire what they appeared to have.

Freedom. Confidence. Swagger.

Sure, I continued to live at home because I attended the local college, not some fancy far-off place. But with the tiny bit of independence I now had, I started staying later on campus than my classes required. Taking time to hang out with my fellow students rather than go home to do my never-ending chores. The chickens could feed themselves as far as I was concerned.

Then I took things one step further and ended up starting down a path I couldn't think of any way to come back from. One afternoon, a bunch of us lounged on the grass of the quad. The intent had been to study, but the joint being passed around made that an impossibility. No, I didn't touch it. I fiddled with the open textbook on my lap every time the thing got within an inch of me. I hadn't gotten that deep into rebellion yet.

"Hey, Bruce, you coming on Friday?" Steve looked my way. When I gave him a blank stare in return, he continued. "Our house," he waved toward a few of the other guys in the group. "It'll be great. Just show up man, major party with everyone."

Not even debating about it for a second, I responded with a goofy grin. "Sure, sounds fun."

I didn't care in the least who 'everyone' might be. Or in how casual a manner the invite had been tossed out. They wanted me to come to an off-campus event and hang out like a normal guy. An occasion which I'd have to lie to my mother about if I truly wished to attend. Because I didn't want to hear any more lectures about the evils of this world. Or what not to do with a lady.

The party wasn't what I'd thought it would be. The loud music and alcohol I'd expected. But the tangy odor of marijuana mixed with cigarettes I hadn't. On second thought, I should've realized what would be going on given who'd invited me. And given what he'd been holding in his hand at the time.

Based on what little I spotted from where I stood in the entry hall, the crowd didn't fit into my world. Most everyone I knew were good ol' boy Texans, Christians who never sinned or made a mistake. Everyone here was the complete opposite. The main room turned out to be a hazy scene of girls dancing rather suggestively. Boys trying to out-drink everyone in the room or be the first to feel up every girl in the place. The scene was frenetic, chaotic, insane.

Thus, within seconds of entering the house, I took in the whole situation, eyes wide open. Then almost turned around as a sense of panic filled every inch of me.

The floor plan was one of those giant open spaces that many newer homes seemed to have. Massive sunk-in living room with green plush carpeting, and heavy orange couches. Dining room with modern plastic white furniture. Green appliances and orange and white tiles in the bright kitchen. All of this melded into one space.

About every inch appeared to be covered with bodies. Apparently, every student on campus had turned up. As I started to spin on my heels back towards the open door, my buddy Steve spotted me. With an arm high in the air, he waved. He marched towards me, zig-zagging through the crowd. Without a word, he pulled me over to the large cooler in the corner of the kitchen, dodging more people along the way.

Yanking open the lid, "Groovy, right?" He yelled above the din of people talking and the deafening notes of some song by the Rolling Stones.

"Sure," I mumbled back as I drew out a beer from the icy depths.

I'd have preferred a soda but that didn't appear to be an option. I'd had a beer or two with my uncles on hunting or fishing trips and hated the stuff. Just didn't see what the big appeal was. It always hit my nose with this horrendous odor, akin to wet manure, and the first sip always bit my tongue with the same saltiness as sweat.

He slapped me hard on the back and then turned to grab some girl's backside before giving her a big, sloppy kiss. They wandered off into the muddled mess in the living room. Joining in the dancing with wild abandon as they crashed into others who gyrated to the beat as well.

I pulled the tab on the can and took a slow sip of my drink. I grimaced at the bitterness of the cheap brew. Glancing around for a place to hide in the madness, I stood my ground as someone knocked into me. Noticing an unused dining chair, I hauled it into a far corner. Trying to be as careful as possible not to hit anyone in the process, I raised it high above my head.

As I planted myself, a plan formed. I'd finish my drink, or at least half of it, and hightail it home where I belonged. I did a slow scan of the entire area, observing the others around me. All the while wondering why in the world they thought this debauchery had any appeal, or might be in the least bit fun, because to me, this looked painful.

It was rather obvious I'd dressed all wrong for this event. Here I sat, neat as a pin in black dress slacks and a light blue button-down cotton shirt. Whereas everyone else looked like hippies. Bell-bottomed jeans, T-shirts, or no shirt for the men. Colorful dresses, skirts, tops, or jeans for the girls. Some of these people I'd seen in class, others I'd never laid eyes on before. On campus, a dress code of sorts had been enforced, a pushing back against the cultural revolution. Thus, in my mind, the party would be the same.

My mistake.

But then, in the middle of the confusion, there she stood. A few feet away from me in the middle of the kitchen, the girl of my dreams had arrived. The one girl here who didn't seem to be drunk or stoned. And she wasn't getting pawed by every guy in the place.

She controlled her space, even if she was this tiny little five-foot-nothing creature. Her face shaped like a small heart, a tiny button nose. These unusual eyes changed from green to hazel to blue as if by magic. Lips a soft pink, curled into a permanent smile giving her cheeks deep dimples.

Yet I didn't know how to approach her, or even if I should. I'd never been on a date, wasn't sure if I'd even talked to a girl who wasn't one of my cousins. I sunk lower in my seat, thankful I'd hid in a corner, unnoticed by most. Nursing my beer, my mind ran through a few of the lines I might be able to say if I found a way to muster up a bit of courage.

'Your peasant skirt is so colorful, with all of those swirls of reds, golds, greens, and purples.' Dumb.

'Your crochet vest is neat, did you make it yourself?' Maybe.

'Your hair is so flat, how many hours does it take you to iron it?' Way too personal.

No, I couldn't do anything of the sort, talking to whoever she might be was out of the question. I watched as she exited the kitchen area. She twirled around the room, floating rather than walking. She put her small hand on this guy's shoulder as she murmured in his ear.

Then she'd flit off to some other guy, flipping her long golden honey hair as she bent to give him a peck on the cheek. Something was different about her, a light, a glow, a sense of happiness. Confident in who she was, what she was.

I desired nothing more than to be in her orbit, if even for a moment. I leaned forward, drawn to her. Resting one of my elbows on my knees, my head propped on my hand, staring for all I was worth. Trying to understand this girl, to get a grip on what made her different from the others around her.

Then she returned to my side of the room, her hand sliding along the edge of the dining table. She looked my way, our eyes locked for a moment. My heart skipped; my whole body tensed. And I failed, I froze completely. I couldn't smile back at her; I couldn't even maintain eye contact.

My head dropped; my lids squeezed tight as my eyes began to water from the pressure. Panting, my body grew weak and I became afraid I might faint. I lost my grip on the cold can in my hand. It clattered to the floor, the beer splashing against my black penny loafers and pant leg. Mortified, I began to stand but a gentle hand on my shoulder pushed me back down.

With no warning, she wriggled herself onto my lap, her arms twined around my neck. My arms remained slack, hanging towards the floor. We held this uncomfortable pose for a moment or two. Her fingers crept up the back of my neck, stroking my short brown hair.

Slipping a finger towards my jawline, she finished by tracing the outline of my lips. I put one hand on her back, tentatively, giving a gentle tug at the woven holes in her soft peach-colored vest. Afraid to touch her, hold her. Wondering how real this creature might be. Or if I'd inhaled so much marijuana smoke from the others that I'd hallucinated her into being.

"You're the only one here not having fun," she whispered in my ear, her warm breath tickling my cheek. "Why?"

Hesitating for a second, unsure of how to frame my response, I took in a deep breath of air. Jasmine wafted into my nostrils, hitting me like a slap. She wore perfume with the same scent as my mother.

My God-fearing mother who had made me swear to never touch a lady until I married her.

My hand dropped to my side again, a burning sensation running through it as if I'd touched a hot stove. Thoughts of my mother's frowning face filled my mind, I tried to focus on something in the room instead. But nothing stood out as something to be considered worthy of my mother's praise. Thus, the whole room blurred as my eyes flickered back and forth. In vain, I tried to get myself out of the mess I'd landed in.

"Doesn't seem like my kind of scene." My gaze returned to look at her, distorting her face as it did. I blinked hard to clear my vision.

My body became stiff as I tensed every muscle. I remained still despite her hand now wandering over my shirt, giving a slight tug on the pocket. She undid the top button of my shirt and I bit my lip hard enough to draw blood. A lone finger dipped inside, winding around my chest hair, a nail scratching my skin. Before I quite became aware of what had happened, her whole hand now rubbed my abdomen.

Most of the buttons had been undone on my shirt without me even noticing it.

We were too close, in too intimate of a position. Things were moving faster than I'd ever thought they should with a girl. Not from any experience I'd had but based on the little information I'd been taught by my mother. I needed to leave before things got out of hand, if they hadn't gone too far already.

"Well, what is?" Even with our close proximity, hearing her words wasn't the easiest thing. The noise from the beating of my heart swooshed in my ears. The deafening music of Cream blared at me from somewhere in the background and it was getting louder by the minute.

"I'm not sure." Turning my head a fraction to get a better look at her face ended up being a mistake. She leaned in at the same time, our lips ended up touching, resulting in a chaste kiss.

Was it an accident? Or had it been something she'd done on purpose? I had no way of knowing. She removed her hand from inside my shirt, patting my cheek. Giving me a wicked little smile, she put her finger to her lips, then to mine. And she hooked me, stronger than any fish on a line. Deep inside me, a pressure built up that I didn't understand. It wouldn't be conceivable for me to leave her side now.

She tugged on my hand, sliding off my lap, and rising to her feet as she did. I followed her lead, heading out the sliding glass backdoor of the house and into the large yard beyond. Even here, no privacy to be had at all. People were lounging in every corner, smoking, drinking, making out. She never slowed down, didn't even seem to notice the others.

Heading towards a metal gate in the far fence, she marched onward. Pushing it open, allowing it to clang shut behind us, she didn't look back. Once in the alleyway, her steps slowed, her tight grip on me released. She tucked her arm in mine, resting her head on my shoulder. We bounced along, awkward but comfortable.

"Better?" She asked when we were a block or so away. Out on one of the main streets of town, under the soft glow of the street lamps, cars rumbling by.

"Maybe. Quieter at least." I wanted to question her as to why I'd been the one she'd picked. So many other boys were better. Dressed hipper, looked happier, had some clue as to what to do with a girl. But fear filled me, leaving me cold. If I dared to question her motives, she'd disappear as fast as she'd come to my side.

"I'm Donna." Her wide, full skirt swished against my legs as we continued to stroll down the sidewalk.

"Bruce." By then we'd rounded another corner, and the local park now lay before us. She'd had a plan all along, she'd been leading me to exactly where she wanted us to be. To her, I was a sheep in need of a shepherd.

Settling on a bench, she snuggled against me. Nothing like Texas in the fall, blazing hot until near Christmas. The back of my shirt soon dampened with my sweat. Despite the heat of the day not having abated yet, her body seemed cool against mine.

She kicked off her leather sandals, flexing her toes in the close-cropped grass for a moment. Whipping her legs up and down, she ended by holding them straight out as she arched her dainty feet. She finished by tucking her toes under her skirt and leaning her head against my chest. My arms wrapped around her as if it were the most natural thing in the world to do. We remained in silence for quite some time, relaxed, content to be in each other's company.

"Do you live here?" Her small hand reached out to draw tight little circles on my thigh. "I haven't seen you on campus much. Not on the weekends, not at night. Seen you around the classroom buildings some."

"Yup, I live where I've always lived. Been here all my life. Raised on a farm right outside of town." Now wasn't the time to mention my family dynamics, my late father, or any other problem in my life. This moment had to be ours and ours alone.

"I'm from up north. Needed to get away from my parents. Drama isn't my thing." Her hand moved upwards and crept a little too close to a place I'd rather it not be.

"What's your thing?" I took her hand in mine, pulling it into the air. Her tiny fingers appeared so childlike in my meaty paw.

"I'm not sure. Came here in a van with a few friends in the spring. That didn't quite work out. Decided to try college. That's not anything close to what I'd thought it would be either. But I'm meeting some great guys, having some fun, and will figure the rest out later." She gave a laugh, long, light. Letting the sound of its tinkling hang on the evening breeze, she continued on laughing. At some cosmic joke only she understood.

As she chuckled, the rise and fall of her body stirred something in me. I began to smile, then gave out a small chortle as well. In a moment, we were clutched in each other's arms, crying from the giggling fit we were in the midst of. Goodness knows what had struck me as being so funny, but letting go felt so good in that moment.

In my life, so few moments of true joy, pure pleasure, unbridled happiness had occurred. Donna had tapped into something deep inside my heart, a need I seldom expressed. To not feel burdened by the pressures at home. To not feel trapped by the mountains of expectations my family had for me. To be my own man, to stand on my own feet for once. To determine my own fate and destiny.

She reached up to wipe away the moisture from the tears now streaming down my cheeks. Her gentle fingers soft on my face. Rising from the bench, she stretched, arching her back and raising her arms high above her head. She looked this way and that, up and down, rolling her head on her shoulders. Then she took off running barefoot across the park toward the pond in the center.

The faint light of the moon shone down on her blonde hair, making it shimmer and glow. Her skirt fluttered in the faint breeze, my angel with a halo and all. Following her, I saw her stop with no warning. I paused as she plopped down at the edge of the water. A lone duck floated in a weaving, meandering pattern leaving a faint ripple behind it. Visible only because of the streak of moonlight reflected on the surface of the small pond, it appeared lost and alone.

Taking the last few strides to her, I stood behind her, stroking her soft hair. She curled into a tight ball, her arms wrapped around her knees. She stared straight into the darkness of the night, well past the pond and the trees. I wondered what she was thinking about, I didn't have any way to know. I'd learned almost nothing about her, her life, for the most part, a complete mystery.

"Do you think I should be like the duck?" She reached her hand up to grasp one of mine, yanking hard.

Afraid I might fall because of her tugging, I dropped to the ground beside her. "What d'ya mean?"

"Return home in the spring." She turned her face to me, her head tilted, her lips drawn down in a frown.

"I'm not sure yet." How should I respond? It wasn't my place to tell anyone what to do. I wasn't related to her. And from what I'd seen in my life, barking orders at someone remained a privilege only parents were allowed to have. "Ask me again next week."

CHAPTER 3

Colorado – Present Day

Warmth filled me as those memories of the early days of my relationship with Donna flooded my brain. She'd brought so much sunshine into my dull world for those few short months. Never again would I experience anything with such intensity as I had with her.

Nancy didn't send chills up my spine; never had. What our relationship entailed, well, I'm not sure calling it love would be fair. At least on my part. So many times over the years I'd wished for nothing more than to walk away, believing that to be best for everyone.

But I couldn't do that to another woman. To another child. No, I had to be a man and face my responsibilities. Be the man everyone believed me to be, wanted me to be, needed me to be.

Not the man I, in fact, am.

Rather be the man I'd created out of nothing.

Taking a few sips of my beer, I let my mind's eye linger a bit longer on that scene at the pond. On how beautiful Donna had looked in the glowing moonlight. Yet, how much of this memory was true? And how much had I made sweet because the passage of time had smoothed the rough edges?

"She sounds like a fantasy." Ryan leaned on the bar, his arms crossed, his eyes focused on something on the other side of the room. He began to tap his fingernails on the wood, playing out an odd tune.

"In a way, I think she was." My voice soft, low, not wishing to spoil the image of my perfect woman.

Donna, my soulmate, the one I should've married.

How many things in my life would've been different if I had? Would it have been possible to find a way to stay in school? Never end up in Nam? Settle down in Texas, become a veterinarian, and live out my days in peace?

Growing old with Donna as we watched our child turn from baby to adult; would we have had a great life? It's not like I hadn't considered all of the possibilities. Or the fact that even if I'd stayed I might still have ended up going to war. Keeping my grades up while caring for a wife and child wouldn't have been easy. Not like I cared either way about being drafted, however, no one asked for my opinion on the matter. At the time, I'd wanted to prove myself to be a man like my uncle. To show myself capable of giving my all for my country like a few of the other local boys were doing. But I do think if we'd gotten married it would've been best for me to have been there to give support to my new bride.

Yet nothing had made sense back then. No move which could've made everyone involved complete.

Not for my mother. Not for Donna. And for darn sure, not for me.

This fantasy of a life with Donna I'd often forced myself to push out of my mind in those early days of Nam. I couldn't think about those what ifs and should've beens. I'd made my bed and now I'd have to wallow in it. Afterward, I did everything imaginable to forget her and what may or may not have ever happened between us. Because Donna couldn't ever be anything more than a fairy tale.

And fairy tales don't come true.

But our child, that remained another matter altogether. So often I'd look at a child who'd be a bit older than my Lisa and wonder. Does that laugh sound familiar? Does he have my eyes? Does she have my nose? Yes, I'm aware the odds of a chance encounter were a billion to none. But my heart didn't care.

And here I'd been given the moment I'd waited for, longed for, wished for. A connection to that long-ago lost child. No, not lost. I'd been the one who'd been lost. Because I'd taken myself out of the equation. A daughter—I'd had a daughter in August of 1968. Part of me wanted to shout it from the mountaintops for all the world to hear. Part of me wanted this bit of information to remain hidden forever.

How much of her mother's traits had my daughter gotten? How much of me? Beyond mere appearances, I didn't wish certain characteristics of mine upon anyone. Did she lean toward being a free spirit, going wherever the wind blew? Or did she pretend problems didn't exist, run away at those times things got too hard?

And now that these thoughts had crossed my mind, I realized how alike the two were. Neither Donna nor I had stuck around to face the challenge that was our child. Not like Donna had a whole lot of say in the matter; I'd pushed her too far. To a place she didn't have but the one option left. I'd known this fact then, even when I tried to deny the truth of the matter.

So, someone had chosen to step up when we failed our child.

Who were those people? Had they been good to her? Had they been kind? Had they provided for her every need? Not for those things that money can buy, but for her emotional needs as well?

Or is that why she now had come looking for me? Did she have a hole in her heart bigger than the Grand Canyon? Did she feel abandoned? Lost, confused, hurt, angry? Was she needing to vent, scream at me for never being around?

So many questions, so many answers I didn't think I'd ever have. I shook my head, my heart breaking at all of these racing thoughts.

"So, Donna cracked open your shell? Turned you from farm kid to…" he paused. "Well, whatever it is you are now. Lumberjack? Doesn't seem like that much of a difference man."

"Bit more to it than that, Ryan. I turned my back on my family for her." I gulped, that sounded so ridiculous when I said it out loud. Because what happened between my mother and I had nothing to do with Donna in the end. "Never mind, suffice it to say I ended up leaving both Donna and my family behind without another word."

"Wait, you're being serious here? You haven't seen or heard from Donna until now?" He leaned towards me; eagerness written all over his face. "Everything you know about her is based on that year in college? Because, man, that was like forever ago."

"She isn't the one who told me I had a kid." I coughed, blinking hard, trying not to cry at the thought that more than likely I'd never see my true soulmate again.

"Uhm, okay. Then who did?" He tilted his head, looking up at the tin-plated ceiling. His brows pulled down as he contemplated the puzzle of my life.

My eyes followed his. The patina on the details in the flowers and swirls had changed the intricate patterns over time, making everything hazy, softer, and muted. This building had stood the test of time. It'd witnessed countless stories and still remained as a silent witness through them all.

My life must be the same. After all, all my faculties remained intact, thus my memories can't be that flawed. The picture of Donna embedded in my head and heart had to be real. I'd destroyed her and everything we'd had by my own selfish act.

"My child." I looked straight at Ryan, firm, strong words.

Despite how simple of a statement it was, so much more remained hidden behind these words. And I didn't doubt for a second he'd start peppering me with more questions at this bit of news.

Instead, he straightened up and spun around, scanning the small space for a moment. Then he bent to reach deep into a cupboard, a few things falling to the floor with pings and thunks which he ignored. The stuff he did manage to retrieve he tossed onto the back counter. He continued to scrounge around in the fridge for a few more items.

"This conversation is going to take longer than I thought. We need something to go with our drinks." He threw these words over his shoulder as he continued his frenetic labor.

After a few minutes, he turned back to me, two plates with toasted sandwiches in his hands. Placing them on the counter, he shifted a bit on his feet, then nodded to himself. Removing his apron, he tossed it over his head into a far corner. Craning my neck, I spotted a pile of other dirty linens in the general vicinity of where it now lay.

Reaching under the counter, he pulled out two bags of chips which he threw near me. After getting two new beers, he placed them in front of the plates. He did one more quick scan of the room before walking around the counter and plopping onto the stool next to me. The thing almost tossed him off. It wobbled for a moment before he steadied it by planting his feet firmly on the floor. Giving me a wink, he shifted a bit, looking down at the ground to ensure he wasn't about to be bucked off.

Without saying a word, he began to munch on his sandwich, sliding a bag of chips his way. When in Rome, it being well after lunchtime and a beer or two in, I might as well chow down as well.

We ate in silence, neither of us doing anything more than enjoying the meal. Which was a far sight better than any meal I ever had with Nancy in all my years of marriage. Not because the food Ryan had just given me turned out to be something gourmet or fancy. No, something else was at play here.

This meal we ate in silence, not a sound to be heard other than those coming from our teeth as we chewed. With my wife, a moment of quiet had always been impossible to have. For the simple reason that Nancy had this habit of talking nonstop during a meal. Well, to be more precise, any time she happened to be awake. To the point that I hadn't any idea how she managed to get a bite in edgewise. Or watch television, listen to the radio, or do anything else.

She shared every bit of gossip about everyone she'd ever met with everyone she met. And for the love of all that was holy, I'd learned to keep my big mouth shut over the years. Because our business wasn't private as far as my dear wife was concerned.

Goodness only knew what she'd do when she learned about my million and one secrets. Heck, she didn't even know I'd been in Nam. Not like she hadn't asked, and more than once over the years. She never understood how I'd managed to avoid the whole thing without being in school. Not for as long as I claimed to have done.

As I reflected more, I'm sure she realized I'd been to Nam. Because she never quite believed the lie about what happened to my hand. Those little jabs about, "What part of the motorcycle did your hand get caught in? The chain, right?" as she'd chuckle and give me a knowing wink. Then point to my side where the scars from the shrapnel wounds were.

When Ryan had finished his lunch, he pushed the remains off to the side. Scratching his chin, he looked down for a moment. "Okay. Well, my gut feeling had been your ex-girlfriend called you out of the blue. All to let you know about your daughter. You know, for some medical reason or something similar. Then you hit me with the adoption bit. Yikes, I'd figured the kid found her mother first."

He tapped out each point as he made them. "But, now, let me make sure I've got this straight. Your daughter, whom you've never met, reached out to you today. No mention of Donna, just you. And instead of having a conversation with her, you decided to hang out with me instead?" His nose scrunched up as he shifted his gaze toward me.

I swallowed hard, the lump in my throat growing by the minute. On second thought, lunch hadn't been such a good idea. The distraction for a while had been nice, but now the whole situation still had to be faced. I poked at a wayward chip crumb; it flipped off the plate. Even the chips I couldn't get rid of.

"Well, it wasn't like she came to my house or anything." I grimaced, not like it mattered how she'd gotten in touch. "She sent me an email. For all she knows it ended up in the spam folder and I never even saw the stupid thing."

"Again, dude, uncool." He yanked my plate, sliding it off towards the side where his now rested. The movement ended up being too forceful and the dish continued on its trajectory. It went flying off the countertop. The sound of it clattering onto the floor caused me to jump in my seat.

I stood. "Excuse me for a moment, nature's calling."

He nodded and pointed towards an open doorway. A dark hallway lay beyond. A neon sign hung on the wall, proudly saying, 're tr o '. Ryan seriously needed to sell this place before it fell down around his ears.

As I entered the hall, a single bulb came on through the magic of automatic lighting. A dim fifteen-watt bulb at the far end, near the 'ex t' sign. If the door to the gents hadn't had a giant picture of a silhouetted man painted in bright white on it, I'd never would've found it in the dark. Lucky for me, as I pushed the door in, another equally dim light flickered on inside the room. Only to reveal a bathroom the worst gas station in the nation would be proud of.

Bits of toilet paper and paper towels stuck to the floor and walls. The sink faucet dripped leaving an ugly green line behind. The porcelain sink itself cracked beyond repair. The urinal was also cracked, to the point I was half afraid to use it. However, after a quick peep into one of the stalls, I did. Because no toilets were to be had as an alternative. How this place had a license to operate was beyond me. I did my business as quickly as possible, washed my hands without touching anything, and got back out to the main room.

When I returned to my seat at the bar, Ryan had cleaned up and fresh beers awaited us. He sat fiddling with his phone, passing the time as he waited for me. I guess the thought hadn't crossed his mind that

I'd walk out when I'd finished in the bathroom. Or that I wouldn't high-tail it out the back door upon spotting it. Nope. He'd assumed I'd be willing to continue our visit like it was the most natural thing in the world to do.

"Bruce, would it be possible for me to see the email?" He shifted his gaze from his screen to me, placing the device on the counter.

"Why?" Nosy little bugger, wasn't he?

"Easy, I want to see what she looks like." He gave me a big grin.

Was he wanting a date? No, that can't be right. My daughter must be twice his age. "Again, why?"

"To get a sense of what Donna looked like of course." He tapped on his phone, slow measured ticks. "Because I'm sure hoping your daughter looks like her, not you. No offense."

I'd slammed the computer closed too fast this morning when I'd first seen that email. Had an attachment with a photo been in it? I shut my eyes, trying to visualize the screen. A complete blank. I couldn't even bring up an image of any part of the email other than those words, 'I'm your daughter.'

Since I'd left both the computer and my phone behind, I didn't have a way to look at the email again. I'd been darn fortunate I'd slapped my wallet in my back pocket when I'd dressed. This had been a habit I couldn't seem to break for love or money. Didn't matter that I almost never went anywhere or bought anything anymore. Still, each day, my pants went on and that wallet went in. Plus, my pocket knife. I'd been carrying that around since my twelfth birthday when my uncle first gave it to me. Not like I used the thing very often either. But it had been a mite useful over the years.

"Sorry, we have two problems here, Ryan. First, I don't know if a photo is in the email. Second, I don't have any way to access my email to find out for sure or not." I gnawed on my bottom lip. Wishing I'd taken a moment to grab the phone off its stand in the bedroom where it rested all night to charge. Yet, in the state I'd been in when I'd fled, out of sight had been out of mind for darn sure.

He chuckled, rising from his seat. "I'll be back before you can blink. We'll look at it together, okay?" Without waiting for my reply, he strode towards the back hallway.

I stared out the lone window which commanded most of the front wall. The rain continued to come down in buckets, large drops ran down the glass in rivers. The building across the street appeared as nothing more than a blurry, wavy form in the foggy, watery haze. Not a single car drove by, no one dared to be out walking on the sidewalk. The town had hunkered down for the duration of the storm.

Ryan's return blocked my view. He plopped a beat-up, chunky, old silver laptop down in front of me. Mine was newer and in better condition. Bit of a surprise, me being the dinosaur in the room.

Opening it, he swiped on the touchpad to pull up a browser—the thing wasn't even a touch screen. "Now what platform do you use? Gmail, Yahoo, what?" He grinned. To him this was so easy.

Panic filled me for a moment—what's my password? When I used my own device, I never had to input it. The form always came prefilled, or it sent me a text to get a code. And I didn't have my phone.

He gave my arm a pat, a comforting smile on his face. With the patience of a saint, he walked me through all of the steps and had me logged on in no time flat. Rather scary finding out how easy it is to gain access to my email without any clue of what the password might be.

Might Nancy have been sitting on the couch reading it at some point this morning as well? Doubt it, she didn't even know the code to get into the computer. She'd always been happy to just keep using her tablet. Seemed rather unlikely she had any of the skillset required to do what Ryan was now doing for me.

When he had finished his task, he pivoted the computer in my direction. "Do your thing dude. I don't know which email to pick. Because, really man, don't you know what the trash can is for? You've got like a million messages here!" He laughed as he waved a hand in front of the screen.

No, I don't delete anything, it might be important later. Yikes, I know, those coupons from Sears and K-Mart I'm not ever going to use. Yet, right at this moment, as I sat there staring at the screen, I hesitated. Allowing my breathing to slow and my heart to calm, I saw his point.

18,244.

I have 18,244 emails in my inbox. How long does it take to remove that many things from your inbox? How had I even noticed Jenny's little note in the middle of this chaos? Yet, my inbox and my life were the same, cluttered to hide my secrets. Which didn't work, as I now knew full well.

Pulling up the correct email, the first thing to catch my eye was the little attachment icon. Right there at the bottom lay a tiny thumbnail picture. Clicking on it, I sucked in most of the air in the room as I watched it enlarge. A gorgeous woman appeared on the screen.

Taking my time, I used the arrow icon to move it in and out, larger, smaller, looking at it in depth. The photo had been taken on a beach somewhere, she wore a blue and white floral dress, no shoes. Her heart-shaped face beamed with a smile, causing a deep dimple on her cheek.

Wrinkles lay in the corner of her light green eyes from squinting in the bright light. She gazed at something down in the sand beneath her feet, one toe in the water. Her shoulder-length blonde hair shone in the sunlight, giving her a glow.

My darling Donna all grown up.

No, not Donna.

Our daughter. But she looked so much like her mother it hurt. The pain hit me, making me realize I'd robbed this precious woman of the opportunity to have her mother in her life.

"You're not okay, are you?" A hand rubbed my back, another patted my arm.

And I didn't give a fig I'd started to sob like a baby as I'd been gaping at the picture. Or that a man I didn't know tried to console me as I did.

Here in this second everything in my life collided, past to present. Meshed into one whole. The thing I'd wished for, longed for, year after year, now had become a reality. I'd seen the face of my child.

For at least one moment in time when this photo had been snapped, she'd been happy. My hope remained that she'd had a great life, filled with joy. My baby had a name—Jenny. She wasn't a faceless, nameless form haunting my dreams any longer.

Would I rip her world to shreds if I dared to respond? What image of her birth parents does she hold? Surely, it's not one of a selfish young man who couldn't handle taking care of anyone other than himself. Will she give me an ounce of grace, even though I deserve none? Or is this as simple as she just wants to meet someone who shares her DNA? To look into the eyes of someone and see the same eyes reflected back?

No easy answers to be found here, my sobs continued as I tried in vain to focus on the image of Jenny. One weekend, that's all it took to create her. I made one stupid mistake, then kept making them long after that, and now, here she is. Wishing for answers as to how she came into being.

"Ryan, what's the dumbest thing you've ever done?" I managed to choke out, my tongue feeling like it'd swollen to twice its normal size and my throat tight.

"What? Besides standing around in this lavish bar of mine for hours? Waiting in vain for all of my millions of patrons to come waltzing in here every day?" He snickered, giving the place a good once over with a critical eye.

Touché.

"Right, I guess I had that answer coming. But come on now. Get serious with me for a moment. What's one giant whopper you did? Say when you were a kid? Or better yet, when you were eighteen or nineteen? There must've been something…" A tip of my thumb brushed against the edge of the photo on the screen. I drew my hand back not wishing to leave a smudge on the image.

"Gosh, that's a toughie." He continued to stroke my back and shoulders as his face scrunched in thought. "I'd have to say lighting the principal's office on fire my senior year."

I choked, trying not to laugh. "Excuse me?"

"Yeah, I'm not on the same level as you. I never got a girl preggers. But I did bring a candle to the principal, we had a lady in charge for your information. Thought I'd do something nice for her since almost everyone gave her such a hard time. However, it rather backfired; I used a campfire lighter to get the thing started. But my hand shook so bad, I waved the thing around and lit the papers on her desk as well."

He chortled as the memory of the event washed over him, clapping me on the back hard. "She leapt up, grabbing the loose pages. And ended up tossing them onto the cleaning supplies being stored on the floor. Which exploded into a fireball about ten seconds later. Guess I should be thankful I only got expelled, not arrested!"

Uhm, young men are dumb. We need more than a few hard knocks in life to get us to wise up some. I'm not responding to that story at all. "At least the consequences of that act were short-lived. My mistake lasted a lifetime."

"I hear ya, dude. I finished out the year right here in the bar, my dad acting as my teacher. Got a GED instead of a diploma. Still, didn't slow me down much, I ended up at a good college." He wriggled his nose. "So, what makes you think creating a life wasn't the right move?"

He had me there, nothing about Jenny's life should be considered a stupid mistake. What I did in response, now that was an entirely different story. "As I look back on things now, I'd have to say the irresponsible thing would be going against what I believed in my heart to be right."

CHAPTER 4

Texas – 1967-1968

I don't know why I'd agreed to give Donna the birthday gift she wanted, asked for, for all intents and purposes demanded. We'd been dating for about two months at that point. It was wild, rash, impulsive. And yet, some small part of me wanted and needed to do her every bidding at that point. Consequences be damned. Rules were made to be broken.

So there I was, mid-November, ready to dive into the deep end and go all the way with Donna. As in going well beyond the few kisses we'd shared. Much, much farther than touching her under her blouse—and discovering, to my surprise, that she didn't wear a bra. Oh my, no, my desire now lay elsewhere. I longed to touch every inch of her from her pretty little toes to the top of her shiny golden head.

I pulled my beat-up old Ford pickup truck up to the curb in front of the house she'd crashed at that week. My hands had almost slipped off the steering wheel as I drove up the street. They were so wet from sweat they'd begun to pucker. My nerves had me shaking so hard, finding the handle to the door became difficult and it took several tries. Thus, I jumped out, leaving the door wide open in my wake.

I glanced at her for a second, as she stood on the front porch, radiant as always. Today she wore a tight lavender short-sleeved sweater paired with a deep purple plaid skirt. To finish the outfit she had on these knee-high white leather boots. She'd pulled her hair back into a loose ponytail, curled over her shoulder. This allowed her large gold hoop earrings to shine in all their glory. Rushing to where she waited, I gave her a quick peck on the cheek. Then, I yanked her small overnight bag out of her hand, heading back to the waiting truck which I'd left running.

"What's your rush, cowboy?" She giggled as she glided behind me. "We've got two whole days ya know."

"Sorry." I tossed her stuff into the bed with mine; I'd cleaned the truck from top to bottom earlier. Didn't want any hay or manure to end up on her or her luggage, nor did I want her to think less of me for being a mere boy fresh off the farm.

Opening the passenger door for her, "I just can't wait to get you alone." I tried to give her a wicked little smile and started to reach out to pat her backside. But pulled my hand back at the last second. We were in public after all, no one needed to see me doing something as brash as that.

I'd booked us a room at a motel a few towns over, lied, and said "Mr. and Mrs." when I did. Just in case anyone asked any questions, I didn't want to ruin Donna's reputation. Hoping beyond hope no one we knew would spot us. Because they'd know it wasn't true.

We drove the whole way in silence. Almost an hour of her soft hand on my thigh and me having a rather difficult time breathing because of it. Her eyes never stopped gazing at me. Her soft body snuggled against mine as she curled up in the middle of the bench seat. Made it darn near impossible to shift gears, turn the wheel or focus in any way, shape, or form.

Oh, how thankful I was to see the sign for the motel up ahead. The pressure from the drive had me wanting to turn around and go home. Now that we'd arrived, perhaps doing something normal should be our next step. Like taking a rather long walk, in a very crowded place, with her not touching me at all.

The motel turned out to be one of those just off the highway, one level, bargain basement, need a room for the night, next to the truck stop, places. The wooden siding a faded, worn green with orange accents. Dead plants in cracked pots on both sides of the dark wooden entrance door that had a worn 'OFFICE' sign hung on it. The large window next to it so streaked with grime, seeing through it was an impossibility.

Turning my head a fraction, I looked down the row of doors which led to the rooms, the concrete walk cracked and uneven. The roof overhang leaned precariously on bent posts. Most of the numbers on the doors hung askew, a few missing entirely. Every car and truck in the lot appeared to be older than mine.

Yup, I'd picked the most expensive motel I'd been able to afford. A total dump.

I entered the tiny motel office, Donna one step behind me. "Mr. and Mrs. Johnson, checking in for the weekend." I declared as proud as could be to the lone person in the place.

I held my head high, ready to defend myself for the lie if need be. Not sure I should've bothered, the room had the reek of decay and decades of smoking. The dark wooden paneling speckled light and dark in a weird wavy pattern. Marks from where the sunlight from the window had faded it. The dark blue carpet had more holes than wool.

The woman sitting behind the counter, fifty going on two hundred. Her dyed blonde hair pulled up high in a beehive, revealing the dark roots. A cigarette hanging out of her lips done up with scarlet lipstick that streaked well beyond her lip line. Her cheeks painted with bright purplish-red rouge, her lashes thick, long, false, giving her more than a bit of a clownish look. The orange checkered dress she wore had holes in it, plus bits of ash from her cigarette had fallen onto her lap.

The clerk took one long look at us, at Donna's naked left hand, but never questioned the truth of my claim.

Well not beyond an under-her-breath grunt of "Being just 'bout to ship out don't make it right." She reached behind her to haul a key off the hook on the wall behind her, not bothering to stand. Sliding it over the desk my way she said, "Don't allow no noise past ten."

She squinted hard, tapping the cigarette on the edge of a freestanding ashtray. Most of the dust missed and landed on the floor. "Room two. Leave the key in there when you're done with your business."

I didn't bother to reply, it was clear she understood what we were doing and why. Though, she had it half wrong. I wasn't about to go to Nam. Back outside, I snagged our stuff out of the truck and took the few steps towards our room. I had my backpack slung over one shoulder, Donna's small case in one hand, the large key in the other. We approached the proper door, and I reached out to put the key in the lock.

She pulled me in close, giving me a lingering kiss. "Thank you."

Not quite letting go of me even as I struggled to get the door open.

Giving the door a kick with my heel to close it once we were past the threshold, I put her luggage on the lone wooden chair. She wrapped herself around me, sliding her hands into the back of my jeans to give a tug at my underwear.

I pulled away. Was I ready for this? No little step this thing we were about to do. Rather it was a giant leap and it wasn't possible to come back from this. However, Donna had asked me over and over for this, taking our relationship further. Marriage so old-fashioned and unnecessary according to her.

"Let me change. Let you relax for a moment." Her finger traced the stitching down the front of my white button-down shirt. A fingernail flicked at one of the buttons towards the bottom where I'd tucked it into my jeans.

My eyes followed her every movement as she pulled a few things out of her bag. She proceeded to do a slow, hip-shaking sashay toward the bathroom. And I didn't move a muscle as I listened to her activities coming from the other room.

Doing a quick scan of the main room, I realized it wasn't any better than the office. My fault for finding the cheapest place I could. I didn't have much in the way of spending money to throw around for things like this. The walls were dull white, the bed a simple brass frame with a tan bedspread. The carpet was a deep green, threadbare, and worn with a weird pattern of where many feet had trod. Door to bed, bed to bathroom, a shiny trail showed each new guest where to walk. A simple table, cracked and scratched, stood next to the chair.

My feet remained glued to the floor as the door opened with a slight creak. She leaned on the frame, one arm raised above her head.

She'd changed into a dark pink, frilly nighty/bathrobe combination. The bottom of the robe so short most of the top of her thighs had become visible to my wandering eyes. The sash tied so loose I spotted the nighty beneath was made of see-through lace. She glided over to me, giving a slight tug on the strap of my backpack which still clung to my shoulder.

"Come on, we can't do anything until you get comfortable." She shifted my arm just enough to take the pack off, placing it on the table.

This all had gone too fast, I'd thought we'd at least wait until after dinner, hopefully well past dessert. "Uhm…" I didn't have any idea what I should or shouldn't be doing. Yet wasn't the man supposed to be the one taking the lead?

She began to undo my shirt buttons, gently guiding me to the waiting bed as she did. Pushing me onto the hard mattress, she leaned into me, planting another long, smoldering kiss on my wet lips. With no warning, she spun and strode to the far side of the bed.

"Why are you so stiff?" She pulled down the covers, plumping up the pillows before snuggling into the nest she'd created. Futzing with the ruffles of her robe, she spread out the bright cloth around her. Resulting in it looking for all the world like she was an angel resting in a pink cloud.

"I think I've changed my mind." Turning my head, I stared at the dark green thick velvet curtains covering the windows. A thin sliver of light shone in the crack where the two halves met. Seeing out into the parking lot an impossibility with such a narrow view. "This is a big deal, are we ready for this?"

"I've been ready since the night we met. It's why I led you to the park." She let out a small giggle. "So we could be alone and let the moment take us wherever it might want us to go. But you're not like other guys and I didn't push things that night."

My head whipped back to look at her. "I'm not your first?"

"I'm not going to kiss and tell." She pouted for a second, twirling a strand of her hair around her finger. "You're the only one that matters to me."

"What if something happens?" I shifted a bit, putting a hand on the bed to steady myself as the room began to spin.

"Like what?" She cocked her head, squinting her eyes in puzzlement.

"I hurt you." Not what I meant at all, but the words I wanted and needed to say I couldn't find a way to express in mixed company.

"You won't. I can take care of myself." She patted the dingy cream sheets beside her, inviting me to her side. "Would it be easier if the lights were off?" Without saying another word, she reached over to the side lamp and pulled the chain. Plunging the room into darkness, I blinked. Except for the faint glimmer emitting from the center of the window, everything now lay hidden.

That small glow called out to me to come back to the world I'd always known. To not go against everything I believed in, everything I'd been taught and raised to be. I knew sex outside of marriage was a sin. I'd heard whispers of what happened to girls who 'got in trouble' and had to leave town in the middle of the night. But I also was aware of how many guys on campus bragged about what they'd done over the weekend. And how forward Donna had been with me.

Yet, up till now, I'd always put a stop to her attempts to do anything that might lead to something like what we were about to do. My heart and my head debated, give in to Donna or continue on in our current state of doing nothing more than holding hands. She hadn't been raised in a strict, Christian home as I had been. There wasn't a line for her to cross. But for me, as a young man, there remained a giant chasm between what I'd been told to be the correct path and what I now sat here contemplating.

In the end, I shifted towards the hand that now slid up and down my back. I slid rather awkwardly towards the head of the bed, taking her into my arms. As I relaxed, I began to lose control of myself. And the more my body tingled with pleasure, the more I didn't care about what I should be doing. She stroked my face with her slim finger, her lips pressing against my cheek.

"Thank you," she bit my earlobe as her fingers tore off my shirt.

As my eyes began to adjust to the dimness, I witnessed her face shift from a tight ball of worry to one that was relaxed, happy, satisfied.

And I allowed her to weave her spell over me as the weekend unfolded.

Over the course of the next several months, we spent as much time together as possible. I'd all but given up going to class except when exams or presentations happened and I had to show up. Each time I'd get a paper or quiz back, I cringed. My grades were sinking, fast. And I lied to my mother—well, to everyone. I didn't care what they wanted anymore, because I craved Donna more than anything else. Didn't seem to matter much either that I might be hanging onto my waiver by my fingernails. War didn't scare me, not sure if it ever had, if someone were to ever have questioned me about it. However, at this moment, what I'd done had made me a man. I felt I could conquer the world.

And it didn't appear to me that my momma had been right about everything after all.

We'd often lay out in the winter sunshine on the grass in the middle of campus. Snuggled together, we'd ignore everything and everyone but each other. Both of us were desperate to find another way to be alone.

But she didn't have a real place to live, rather she crashed with this friend or that. And I lived at home. No way for me to bring Donna anywhere near my mother.

Thus, Christmas had been a nightmare. For three whole weeks, we couldn't see each other because I refused to invite her to my mother's house. Instead, we'd whisper to each other during long phone calls. She didn't want to be overheard by her roommate of the moment and I didn't want to be overheard by my mother.

More often than not, she'd ask why I refused to have her visit. But I didn't know how to find the words to say how hurt my mother would be if she learned what had happened in that motel room. No, it would be impossible to get my two favorite women in the same room together.

Yet, Donna's life and mine were entwined now because of the fleeting moment we'd shared. No, the experience hadn't been repeated. I didn't see how to come up with another excuse to leave my mother alone again.

My first lie of spending the weekend hunting with some buddies hadn't gone over well. Not when I hadn't come home with some deer meat. Because of course, Donna and I hadn't ever left the room and my gun hadn't ever left the truck. The weekend had been for just us, we'd spent it wrapped in each other's arms. We were lucky we'd managed to have those two magical days where our two souls had become one.

Thus, our time together became more about sharing our dreams as we'd talk for hours. Kissing became the best we could do—well, that and a whole lot of groping. Not like we were the only ones on campus making out in public. To be honest, we might have been the most chaste couple out on the quad.

She'd considered joining the peace movement. I discussed my hopes to have my own practice as a vet someday, treating horses and cows. Maybe dogs, but not household pets. I wanted to help farmers and ranchers. Not people who didn't understand animals were here for a purpose and not to be used as playthings.

Then, a few days before Valentine's, Donna insisted we needed to spend some time alone. Even if but for an hour or two, off campus, we needed privacy. We skipped class, as always. But this time, we headed out of town in my truck toward nowhere in particular. She didn't reach out for me as she always did, she sat silent staring out at the cows and fields as we drove. I parked along a river bank, under the trees for a hint of shade.

As I turned toward her, I noticed a look of pain in her eyes. My gut told me she was leaving me, the time had come for my bird to fly away. Either she'd go home or somewhere else far away, but this moment would be our last.

"I love you. With all my heart and soul, Bruce, I've grown to love you. I didn't expect that. Did you?" She gave me a sideways look through her lashes, her head tilted a bit to the side.

Why would she say that? Especially since this isn't what her body language was throwing my way right at that moment. "Sure baby. I've been having fun with you." I started to reach out my hand but she recoiled and I pulled back as well. Guessing she needed to hear the words in return, I managed to get out, "I love you too." Not sure what I'd done wrong to lead us to the point of her being angry.

She picked at the brown paisley print of her dress, biting her lip. "I'm pregnant."

My hand slapped the steering wheel, then gripped it tight. My head lowered to lay on the wheel, my eyes closed, my breathing labored. This couldn't be happening, how had we made such a mistake? We'd only been together for one weekend. I raised my head just enough to see her, "No. I thought you said you knew how to take care of yourself."

"It's fine. You don't have to do anything." She tipped her head down, her long hair falling over her face like a curtain.

Sitting up straighter, I wondered if she really had meant her words. That I bore no responsibility here. "Then why tell me anything at all?"

"So you won't wonder later." She looked right at me, her eyes blank, ice-cold blue. "I'm not expecting anything from you, I don't need anything."

"Perfect. Because I'm not going to marry you if that's what you were thinking. You can't trap me with your declaration of love." I shifted my weight towards the door, trying to create as much space between the two of us as possible. Not like the cab had more than a few feet of room; each breath I took in filled my lungs with the scent of jasmine from her perfume.

"I get that. Yeah, marriage ain't my thing either. I don't want to be tied to anyone or anything." She rubbed her stomach in small circles with the tips of her fingers.

Odd thing to say, what'd she think a child was? From what I could tell, a child was an anchor holding its parents firmly to one spot in the world. Everything you do means nothing anymore. Not unless your offspring is at the center of every decision you make. As I watched her caress her belly, it dawned on me how much she wanted this child.

What her first words in this conversation had meant. What she'd wanted me to say in response. How much I'd failed her at this moment.

Still, this wasn't going to be my problem, she couldn't force me into something I didn't want. Working my fingers around the plastic bumps on the wheel, I swallowed hard. Because as much as I wished to ignore what now grew inside of Donna, that would be impossible. I'd created this particular dilemma we'd landed in, I had to man up and fix it. Pain hit me like a brick.

I couldn't stay here anymore. Not in my truck. Not in college. Not in my hometown. Not under my mother's roof.

My brain worked overtime to find a way out of this mess. A way to help Donna out of this jam without being tied to a kid. We weren't the only two young people who'd ended up in this particular quandary. I didn't make any money working on the family farm and she couldn't live at my house without me marrying her. My mother would never allow that.

We could take off for Dallas or Houston, blend in with the crowd. No, I'd never find a job good enough to pay for more than a single tiny apartment. One of us would be homeless or we'd end up together. We couldn't shack up together, expecting to live in sin forever. I couldn't do that do Donna, every inch of me screamed that I'd disrespected and dishonered her enough. Not to mention my mother would discover the truth at some point. And she'd drag us home to face the consequences of our actions and make me live with the shame for the rest of my life.

My dreams were now going up in smoke.

I'd wanted to get off the farm, make something of myself. I'd also wanted to cut loose and have some fun, be like the other guys. But now my plans weren't to be. All because of one weekend of pleasure I shouldn't have indulged in. In this moment, it became clear how much of a man I wasn't. I'd wanted to experience all that life had to offer but I now couldn't face the consequences.

A baby.

Squeezing my eyes tight, they began to water. Because something else came to me from the dark recess of my mind. Vietnam. My grades were horrible, flunking out remained a real possibility. If I wasn't in school, the draft also remained a very real possibility. Yes, I wanted to get away from here. Yes, I didn't particularly care how. And a solution to everything came to me in a flash.

I stared at her, my eyes as cold as hers. "I'll join the army. I hear the hazard pay from the war isn't half bad. Send you some money so you don't have to worry."

I couldn't handle a baby, so why did I think something as huge as Vietnam would be any better? Not sure. But a little nudge in my brain told me that fighting a communist had to be easier than a screaming baby at two in the morning. And since it looked like I'd end up in the war no matter what I did, might as well bite the bullet and do it on my terms.

"No!" She reached over, dug her fingernails into my arm, deep into the flesh leaving red marks behind. "You can't do something hateful like that, it'd undo all the love we share!" Tears started to run down her face, connecting the dots of her freckles.

"I can't stay here. I'd have to leave school anyway to work to support you, to be able to provide for all the things a baby needs. Might as well do something important, something only a man can do. Haven't you heard all of those reports about what we're trying to do over there?" I tried in vain to pull her hand off me, her grip tightened in response.

"If you do, I never want to hear from you again, Bruce. Do you hear me?" She released me, a finger now wagging in front of my face. "I want my child to only ever know peace, love. You can't be bringing any of that hate anywhere near him! I don't need anything from you, not now, not ever!"

"Wanting to fight for your country is honorable, noble, right? I've heard all about it from my uncle!" I yelled as she put her hands over her ears, humming to herself to drown out my voice. "And it's a darn sight better than those hippies you wanted to join! Those peace and love crazies hate everyone who ain't them! That isn't love and you know it!"

"That was then, this is now! War ain't what it used to be!" She screamed back. "Which is what my friends are trying to get everyone to understand! If you want to fight, fight for us, for our child. Stay here and do what's right…" She deflated as she shifted her attention back to me, her hand drifting down to rest on her lap.

I didn't wish to continue this argument, it seemed rather obvious to me it'd lead to nowhere good. We weren't ever going to agree on this subject and now she'd ended up sounding a bit like my mother. I cranked the truck engine. Gunning it as I took off, the ping of gravel hit the sides and sprayed everywhere behind me.

Driving back towards town, I twisted the knob on the radio to turn it up as high as it would go. Some stupid country tune about boots being made for walking. Sounded rather fitting if you asked me. In the end though, it didn't matter to me what song played. I wanted to drown out any possible chance of further discussion between us.

Because I didn't see any way to fix the bridge we'd just blown up. I slammed the brakes as I approached her home of the moment, stopping well short of the walkway. And I didn't care in the least.

She hopped out, slamming the door behind her. Storming up the path, leaving a dust trail in her wake. I didn't even watch her for more than a second before I peeled off down the street.

I didn't go home that afternoon. I drove around for the rest of the day instead. Camped out somewhere for the night, not caring in the least where I'd ended up. My mother couldn't ever know about the shameful thing I'd done. Donna wanted more from me than I was willing to give. My gut reaction remained the best path forward.

Man up, provide for both my girl and my mother.

In the morning, I went straight to the nearest recruitment office. Told them I didn't want to wait for my number to be pulled anymore, to send me now. And I put my feet on a path it'd be impossible to come back from.

CHAPTER 5

Colorado – Present Day

I closed the lid of the computer and pushed it away from me. I couldn't look at that photo for a second longer. The grief it caused had now become too much. Ryan slid it further off to the side, not saying a word as he did. We sat in silence; I guess neither of us wished to be the first to respond to what I'd shared.

"You could've gone back that day; told her you were sorry. I'm sure you didn't do as much damage to your relationship as you believed you had." Ryan stared off into space, his face bunched up like he needed to sneeze, his eyes half closed. "But, yeah, I get it. Trust me, I do. I lived in Florida before moving back here. Had a girl, nothing serious but we were having some fun. And I think she's part of the reason I can't make up my mind about this darn bar." He scratched the side of his head, taking in the mess around him. "She got all excited about my inheritance. Thought with the money we'd finally get hitched. But I didn't know that's where we were going. Ya know?"

I didn't have any clue how to respond. Yes, I could've said

something trite like, 'Well, all men are pigs' and given him a free pass. It's not like he'd gotten his girl knocked up like I had. Or at least, it didn't sound like a baby might be out in the universe with Ryan's DNA just waiting to be found.

In the end, I gave a slight nod, feeling as if the question had been meant in more of a rhetorical sort of way.

"But you, you got overheated because you got slapped with the unexpected. Sure, you should've stayed, worked things out with Donna. But in the end, it sounds like you were trying to man up in your own haphazard way. Do the right thing. Yes? Did you try to get ahold of her and send money later? Or did you really run and never look back?" He tugged on his chin, his face twitching as his mind raced with all kinds of thoughts, I was sure. "And is that why you called this a mistake?"

Hard to answer that set of questions. I'd been a rash, impulsive boy. Not thinking straight, or being in the right frame of mind back then, I didn't want to face my mother. I didn't want to have to explain to her why I'd gone against everything she'd taught me about how a man should act. In the end, I lived in fear of that for years, knowing full well how ashamed of me she'd be if she ever learned the truth of what I'd done. Not only had I gotten a girl in trouble, but then I'd abandoned her.

Sure, that hadn't been my exact intention at the time.

I hadn't treated Donna like a lady from rather early on in our relationship. I hadn't done what I had been raised to believe the right thing to do was when faced with pregnancy. Nor had I wanted to tell my mother about me throwing her wish for me never to go to war out like so much trash.

I think my uncle would've understood. After all, he always tried to put my mother in her place. And I'd been the one child in the family to show any interest in his war stories. Over the years I'd asked so many questions about his medals, his uniform, his photos from France and England.

But I still wouldn't have been able to stomach my mother heaping so much guilt onto me. I'd done enough of that on my own.

The truth was, I'd never gone back to the house I'd grown up in. No long, drawn-out, sad goodbye, one in which I would've left my mother in a puddle of tears. No, instead I choose to take the coward's way out. I'd called on the phone to say where I'd left the truck, that the keys were under the front seat.

In my heart I told myself I'd stand before my mother someday; I'd explain everything to her from start to finish. How I'd failed her from the moment I'd set foot on campus and continued to be a disappointment to her for so many reasons. But I never did tell her the whole story. Because I never saw her again.

And I should've. At more than a few points over the years, I should've made contact. But one look into my mother's eyes and the secret I held about the baby would've been out. No way would she have ever forgiven me, no matter how many times I might have begged.

And now it was impossible to even try. My mother lay buried in the same Texas dirt my father did. Yup, the internet is a wonderful thing. I'd been cyberstalking my family for a while now.

Not exactly sure why, or if I had a plan when I first looked at the site for my hometown newspaper. But I'd discovered my uncle had turned into a bit of a big deal. Ended up owning half the county, from farms to auto dealerships to the grocery store. My cousins now ran this empire because my uncle is also long dead and gone, buried in that same dirt as my parents.

Thus, I learned about my mother's death within a reasonable amount of time. I also became aware of the funeral arrangements before she had even been taken to the mortuary. Yet, I didn't do a damn thing with this tidbit of information. Not like anyone would've wanted a ghost to show up at my mother's funeral.

As for Donna, she deserved better than me from the moment we first met. But I did list her as the beneficiary on the paperwork from the army all those years ago. If anything would've happened to me, heaven forbid, I had that covered. She would've gotten every last dime that Uncle Sam might wish to hand out to my surviving family.

Beyond that, I think in the back of my mind, yes, my plan had been to find her after my hitch was up. In the end, too many things happened in such a short period of time. And for me, every notion of any kind of 'real' life became impossible to comprehend.

Upon my return from the other side of the world, upside down became my new normal. I've never once tried to find Donna on the web. My gut told me the best thing to do would be to leave her in peace, to let her live out her life as she saw fit. And to leave my memories of her intact. Something I now regretted, because pretending something doesn't exist doesn't make it so.

"Ryan, Nam, well, uhm…" I hesitated; how to put this without trashing those other men I'd served with? "Look, your father's experience in the Gulf can't and shouldn't be compared to mine."

"Because of the protests and stuff?" He patted my shoulder, giving me a slight smile.

"More because of the 'stuff.' How much do you know about Nam?

The real deal, not that BS from television and movies." I began to drum on the countertop. Stopping, I glanced down at what remained of my left hand.

Most of the time, I kept it clenched because even I didn't want to face the missing digits. The memory of that night so long ago still haunted my dreams. At this moment, I splayed it out before me. As I gazed at the rough white line of scaring along the edge from wrist to middle finger, I ached. A chunk the size of about one-third of my hand was missing, left in a million little pieces in Nam. All because I'd been at the wrong place at the worst possible moment.

And I'd been the lucky one.

"Enough to know that war wasn't about communism." He pointed to his father's picture on the wall. "But what war is truly about what the government says it is?"

Fair point.

"Yeah, well, I spent more time wandering around Texas training to go to Nam than actually in Nam. Which, if you ask me, was a good thing. Nam, okay, how do I put this?" I scratched the corner of my eye, "As one buddy of mine put it, 'It was the only time in my life I wasn't prepared to face what I'd find.' Because none of our training ended up being good for anything we'd see in country."

"That bad?" He winced.

"Ever hear of a litter obstacle course?" I waved my hand at him.

"A what?" He leaned in, wanting to learn more.

"Trust me, in war, you don't need to know how to run with a litter while jumping over tires." Visions of Fort Sam filled my head. And of the many men I'd run into during my months of being shuffled from one post to another.

CHAPTER 6

Texas – 1968

The war machine ground on daily in the 1960s. Feeding new recruits into an endless stream of destruction, spitting them back out maimed or dead. From the moment I entered the Army office to announce my desire to join up to the day I returned from Vietnam, I had little say in what I did, from what I wore, to what I ate, to when I slept. But that first decision remained mine and mine alone.

"Son, are you sure?" The gruff man behind the desk asked more than once. His uniform neat and tight, not hiding the fact he had a barrel chest and the muscles of someone who exercised daily. "You can wait for your number to be pulled, you know."

"I don't wish to get into my reasons. Send me, I've been to college, studying vet medicine, I'm ready." I returned his stare.

"Sign here, then go home for a few weeks." He pushed a form my way.

"No. It's now or never." I put a hand on the paper, starting to slide it back to him.

"Got a death wish?" He tapped his pen on the desk, the rap loud in the confined space. "Not like that's a bad thing, given where you want to go."

"No. Just want to do something honorable for a change." I didn't blink.

"I'll get the bus voucher while you put your John Hancock on the page." He dug into his desk for a moment.

Waiting for him to produce this other piece of paper, I remained still. Once I spotted him holding something that said, 'Greyhound,' I snagged a pen. With no hesitation at all I scratched my name on the proper line.

At the bus station, I parked the truck as close to the office as possible. After tucking the keys under the seat, I ran my hands over the top of the door for a moment. This vehicle represented a tiny sense of freedom for me, the ability for me to do what I wanted. To not be under my mother's watchful eye every moment of every day. Now, I'd give it back to her for safekeeping until my return from the other side of the world.

Taking slow, measured strides to the pay phone, I put in a dime. Spinning the wheel to the proper numbers, I called the farm.

One of my cousins answered. "Hello?"

My heart squeezed—was it a good or bad thing that it wasn't my mother? But our door didn't have a lock, our family came and went as they pleased. The same thing could be said about my aunt and uncle's place. I'd drop in unannounced all the time as well. Family was family. We ate together. We worked together. We were supposed to be buried together.

"Hey, it's Bruce. I don't have time to explain but tell Mom that the truck's at the bus station. The keys are under the seat. Send someone to pick it up. Okay? I'll call again later to explain more." I hit the glass wall with an elbow, rushing to hang up the receiver.

"What?" The voice was faint since the phone was almost back in the cradle, but I didn't care to continue this conversation. I'd spill the beans for sure if I said even one word more.

Thus, I hung up as quickly as possible, before the truth of where I was going came out.

Taking my seat on the bus to Houston, I stared out the window at my hometown. Deep inside, even then, somehow, I think I knew I'd never return. I drank in these last views of the place I'd always called home.

The hardware store I'd get nails from to fix the floorboards that always seemed to be loose in the house; the feedstore we sold the baby chicks at when we had extras, or got hay during those years we didn't get enough rain; the mom-and-pop grocery for all those little things you can't grow on a farm, like sugar, flour, laundry soap; the Five and Dime shop where I used to get ice cream floats and penny candy with my friends.

My high school which I'd graduated from less than a year before. A flash of my mother's proud face as she adjusted the cap on my head hit me about then. She'd have nothing to be pleased about anymore.

As we pulled out down Main Street, we headed toward the highway. Tears dropped down my face onto my faded red T-shirt. Fifty miles. I'd never been much more than fifty miles from where I'd been born. I'd never been to Houston before. I'd never been in another state before. My whole world had always been here in this tiny town. And while I'd always craved the outside world, this isn't how I wanted to escape small-town life.

Hour upon hour, I stared out the window. Watching most of Texas crawl by, small towns, fields, cows, oil rigs, whatever. Night came, a driver change happened as we all sat waiting inside a station. I didn't care where we were, and I ignored the rumbling of my stomach; something in me shifted during that journey. Already my heart ached because of all of the wrong choices I'd made. Knowing the pain my mother would be feeling at this moment as she came to the realization I'd fled. Knowing the loneliness Donna would be facing as she carried a child alone.

The next day, upon our arrival in Houston, I asked a kind person at the station for help. She pointed me in the right direction to the hotel listed on the paper I'd been given at the recruitment office. Only a few blocks away, I found the place easy enough. The city bustled with cars, more people than I'd ever seen in my life. Not to mention the tangy, foul odor of rotting garbage coming from the piles in the alleys. Dodging it all, I marched with purpose to the proper street.

The brick building stood before me, massive, solid. Not anything like the motel I'd taken Donna to. I entered a lobby area with a tile floor, dark blue walls, chandelier hanging from the ceiling. Dark wooden stairs led up toward the unknown, brightly lit from a large window high above. Turning, I approached the lone occupant of the large space.

The man at the front desk didn't give me the slightest glance. "Name?"

He then handed me a key with my room number on the tag.

I pocketed the key and headed back outside. I'd spotted a clothing shop about a block back—I'd need some underwear at the very least since I'd left home with nothing. Well, I did have my pocket knife and my wallet; what good they'd do me I wasn't sure. The paper I held also mentioned a few places to eat at, one of which I'd noticed on the corner right next to the hotel.

After making a few small purchases, I ate a less-than-satisfying dinner. Wandering back to the hotel, I settled into my room for the night. The room also turned out to be nicer than the one at the motel I'd taken Donna to. The large room had been done in creams, golds, and reds. An oversized couch had been placed in such a way that you could either watch the television or look out the two windows. The bed had plush pillows and a down comforter.

However, relaxation wasn't possible for me. And not just because of the noise from the other guests, which was considerable and became worse as the night wore on. At one point, I popped my head out the door, only to see various young men drunk, high, or whatever running half-naked up and down the hallway.

Ladies leaning on the dark paneled walls laughing at these antics. All dressed in skin-tight clothes that left nothing to the imagination. At some point in the middle of the night, I heard several thuds. Looking out the window I realized things were being thrown out into the alley below.

No, my thoughts remained on my mother. And the letter I spent the night trying to write. By morning, one lone sheet of hotel stationary remained. The rest lay crumpled in the trash bin beside me. All or nothing, and nothing wasn't an option. My mother deserved to know where I'd ended up even if I never revealed the 'why.'

My dearest Mother,

I'm sorry, I know this isn't what you wanted for me. But it's the best path for me. As I write this, I'm in Houston. However, I doubt I'll be here for more than a day or two. I'm not sure where I go from here but I'm sure it won't be long before I'm in Vietnam.

Don't worry, I'll do everything I can to keep myself safe. To come home in one piece. To return to the farm and pick up right where I left off. I'll even go back to college and finish my degree.

But I'm a man now, I have to stand on my own two feet. Do what's right. I know there's no way you'll ever understand. Someday maybe I'll get the opportunity to try to explain what happened. To tell you why I made this choice, even though I know it's the last thing you wanted me to do.

In the meantime, don't worry about me. Your job is over. I have to take care of myself.

Your loving son,

Bruce

My final attempt left a lot to be desired, yet I didn't have any time or paper left to try again. Because despite the fact it was four in the morning, the phone rang, a faint voice on the line. "Time to wake up. Get your butt to the induction center in thirty."

Stuffing my missive in an envelope, I addressed it. Stopping at the front desk on my way out, I asked for a stamp. The guy sitting behind it was still the same one from the day before. He didn't look at me or say anything, simply put his hand out. I handed him the letter, hoping he'd do the right thing and mail it for me. Not having any idea how trustworthy the man might or might not be, I didn't have any options. I had to have faith in him to do the right thing.

Other young men like me were trickling through the lobby, heading out into the pre-dawn. Various skin tones, dark mahogany to ghost white. We represented every corner of America. Most clutched small suitcases or satchels. I had my shopping bag from the day before, which seemed rather foolish. I should've purchased a case of some kind to put my undies in but now I didn't have time for that. We proceeded down the street in an uncoordinated wave, swishing this way and that. So many of the others barely able to stand after their night of debauchery.

Arriving at the center, we were quickly divided into smaller groups and sent this way and that. Someone barked an order at my group to undress. Then someone who claimed to be a doctor gave us all exams. He shook his head at some, sending them to one side. I guess I passed— I got a plane ticket to El Paso.

Which rather confused me. What in the world was the Army's plan? So far, I'd been on a bus, in a hotel, had a physical, and now apparently needed to go somewhere else. How many men did they lose in this giant shifting about from one place to another with no rhyme or reason?

Yet, whenever I tried to ask a question, I got yelled at. One thing I knew for sure, the Army didn't like me having a clue as to what might happen next. So, I got on the plane with a bunch of other guys I'd seen during my rather brief time in Houston.

As I watched Texas weave in and out from between the clouds, I reflected on my journey. And about how long this shuffling around my home state would continue. Nerves were now getting the best of me. A lack of sleep and lack of food contributed to my general state of unease.

But at some point after the physical, I'd found myself in a small room with a few of the other men from my group. And we'd stood in a line, straight and proud as we solemnly swore we'd support and defend the Constitution against all foreign and domestic enemies. Plus, we'd obey the orders of the president and our officers. And we'd abide by the Uniform Code of Military Justice.

It didn't seem possible for me to take anything back now. Say, 'Oops, I'm sorry, I made a mistake' and that now I wished to go home. An oath had to mean something. Funny I hadn't wanted to say the vows of marriage. Yet I ended up committed to something a whole lot more serious. And that weighed much more heavily on my heart.

On the walk from the airport to the base, something I remembered well from every county fair hit my nose: spice and the sweet smell of corn roasting. Tacos. My mouth watered at the thought. I stopped to buy a few.

A pretty lady in a multicolored striped dress had set up shop at the edge of an alley. She had a fire going in a small barrel cut in half, flipping tortillas resting on a grate over the top of the barrel. Meat grilled on another impromptu grill.

She said something I didn't understand—my Spanish had never been great. I pointed to the meat and tortillas, and she nodded in reply. Rolling up my tacos in foil, she handed them to me as I passed her a few bills. She tried to give me some money back, but I shook my head no.

Munching as I continued along my way, a few of my fellow soldiers looked at me. Squinting at me, probably wondering why I'd be crazy enough to buy food from a Mexican on the street. But this is Texas, my turf, goodness only knew where they were from. Savoring the food, knowing it might be my last taco for a while, I didn't care what the other guys thought. For a moment, I needed this little slice of normal.

For days on end in El Paso, I endured the humiliation of being prepped for military life. Which meant a lot of things. Like getting my hair cut, at my expense because, no, the Army didn't pay for that. Getting fitted for my uniform and being told I'd been 'fat' and out of shape. Getting vaccinations, lots and lots of them.

Plus, all of the tests to determine my MOS—Military Occupational Specialty. One small spark of hope did manage to appear; an officer noticed on some form that I'd been in college studying medicine. I didn't bother to repeat my previous statement from the recruitment office: I'd been majoring in *veterinary* medicine. But well, I'd given up talking back to officers at that stage of the game. I rolled with anything any of them had to say.

At the end of all of this, I'd been handed another bus pass, this time to San Antonio. At this rate, the war would be over long before I'd ever get out of Texas. Another walk through another town in Texas, the Army's way of keeping us on our toes, I guess. My first view of Fort Sam Houston was a grassy field leading to a rock wall with a tower standing proudly behind. It seemed to be something from another time, so out of place given the current situation. Standing for a moment, I hoped I'd be here a while. The place gave off an aura of calm, peace, almost a sense of relaxation. Of course, those feelings were short-lived.

I settled into my assigned barracks, after learning that for the next eight weeks I'd be here for basic training. I'd be taught to salute, march, shine my shoes, polish brass, and exercise until I'd become a lean, mean, fighting machine. The day would start at 4:30 a.m., no late risers allowed. Formation at five, a perfect line a must, no yawning allowed. Breakfast at six, eat fast because it lasts for exactly thirty minutes. Then training, training, training, and lunch and/or dinner at some point during the day. Lights out at 9:00 p.m. Rinse and repeat, day in and day out.

My group wasn't destined to be infantry, no, we'd all have training for other things after basic. I'd be given medic training next. Thus, our drill instructor understood that basic remained a formality that most of us didn't need. Because of this, he used humor more often than not. He'd order us to 'drop and give a hundred'—push-ups, that is. Though, he'd throw us a wink and a smile as he did so.

Even though it was now early March, the heat came in waves. Being from the area—well, almost—it didn't bother me. However, most of the other men weren't from the South. The barracks weren't air-conditioned, the windows didn't open more than a crack. With that many bodies in such a small space, the heat and humidity created more than a few heat rashes on the uninitiated. Complaining only got you an extra five-mile run in the heat or a few hundred extra push-ups, resulting in more than a few dropping from heat exhaustion or stroke.

By graduation, we'd toughened up somewhat as a group. We'd become something of a unit, bonded a bit as we'd settled into the routine of Army life. I'd been one of the few who'd been here by choice. Most were draftees, of course, boys who'd become men because they were forced to due to the draft lottery. Yet the fact remained, the Vietnam War was becoming less popular by the day.

And the Tet Offensive had a lot to do with that. Being isolated on various bases because of being shuffled around as we had been, we'd heard little when the news broke that February and March. Rumors had gotten around, whispers here and there. Babies slaughtered in their cribs. Women tortured or worse. The innocent victims outnumbered the guilty.

What caused us to realize something major was in the wind, were the protesters outside the gates of the base. Their numbers swelled during those eight weeks of our basic training. It didn't take much to figure out something had shifted in the American psyche. This war killed those whom it shouldn't have. We Americans might well be the bad guys in this fight.

As the end of our training drew near, many were now discussing ways to evade their service. Should we simply not return after graduation from basic? Get injured? Find a way to get to Canada? The talk swirled each night, hypothetical for the most part. But the fact remained, some of these men I came to believe I'd never see again. Because, for them, going AWOL had now become the lesser of two evils.

During those few days of liberty between basic and advanced training, I chose to remain on base. No reason to return home and face the emotions my mother might be dealing with. Anger? Hurt? Betrayal? Sadness? Whatever it might have been, I had enough to deal with in my own heart and mind.

By the end of those eight weeks of hard physical exertion, my soul cried out to me about how much I'd hurt Donna. My reaction to her pregnancy had been the opposite of what she'd wanted. Her first words in that conversation had been, 'I love you,' but I had been afraid to respond in kind.

She wanted this baby we'd somehow managed to create. However, the reality remained, by leaving her alone I'd forced her into a corner from which a way out wasn't possible. This was 1968. She didn't have anyone to support her. She couldn't be a single mother and survive in this world with no help.

Had she gone to one of those homes for unwed mothers I'd heard whispers about? Because after what she'd shared about her parents I didn't see her turning to them for assistance of any kind. And I'd never even told her my mother's name, much less introduced the two of them. Thus, the idea of them getting together to raise the child seemed rather out of the question.

And as for other options? Yes, I'd heard rumors of ways to get rid of babies in illegal manners. Doctors or nurses with little or no scruples who didn't care about the unborn. Yet, this was something I didn't quite picture Donna being willing or able to bring herself to do. Not given the look of pain in her eyes as we'd spoken that final time. Or the way she'd caressed her belly.

The creature growing inside of her had already wormed its way into Donna's heart. Thus, one solution remained. Donna would have to give the baby away to strangers. What would that involve? Would she have to reveal who the father had been?

The day after graduation, I sought out the base chaplain. Finding him in a small office at the chapel, I hesitated at the door. Unsure how much to say, how to ask my questions without looking like a cad.

He looked up from the book he'd been reading as he sat at his desk, glancing at me as I stood before him wringing my cap into a ball. "Son, park yourself before you pass out." He gestured to the chair opposite him, "Got your orders to ship out?" He nodded with a faint, warm smile.

Sinking into the wooden chair, I gazed at the desk rather than the man. Papers littered the top, the book of course turned out to be a Bible. The open passage one filled with red lettering, New Testament, one of Christ's sermons no doubt. "You Catholic?" I blurted out, first thing to pop into my head and not even relevant to my needs at the moment.

"I can be." His voice soft, low.

I looked at his round face, his hair grey, his dark eyes lined with worry lines the same as my mother's. "I've got this friend, oh…" I bit my lip, fibbing to anyone was a sin, lying to a priest had to be well beyond that. I changed course and rushed on. "What happens at those homes for unwed mothers?"

He twisted his fingers together, then rested his elbows on the desktop and put his chin on his hands. "Ah, I see. Well, young man, generally, the women are well cared for before their time comes. If it's run by Catholic charities, then the sisters pick a loving home for the baby. Once the baby's born, it's immediately placed into the arms of those loving adoptive parents."

I gripped the arms of the chair hard, digging my nails into the polished wood. "What about the father?"

His face tightened for a moment, his eyes narrowing. "He doesn't have to become involved at all. Most young women never mention who he, in fact, might be." He coughed, covering his mouth for a moment. "Do you need to go to the confessional, my child?"

I panicked. No matter how I answered, this man already understood what I'd done. "Uhm…"

"Son, you're not the first, nor will you be the last I've heard something similar from. You shouldn't carry this burden alone. Before you ship out, let this be one less weight on your heart, your soul. You can't undo the past, you can't right this wrong. But you can move forward and never make the same mistake twice."

He reached out a hand towards me, a gesture of forgiveness and acceptance. "You also can make the most out of what you're given each day from now on. But you have to choose in your heart to do so."

I wasn't ready to receive his gesture or his advice. My feelings of guilt and shame were too strong to be broken so effortlessly by such simple words. Shaking my head 'No,' I pinched my lips tight as I rose to my feet. My breathing came so rapidly that my head began to swim, and I almost sat back down.

Instead, I spun towards the door. Without looking back, I double-time marched out of the building. This couldn't and shouldn't be so easy. All I had to do to escape responsibility for a child was walk away as I'd done? Then never do anything like that again? No, I had to do something more to atone for my sin of premarital sex. And I'd done much more than that. I'd run into the willing maw of the Army, a place that'd accepted me because they needed bodies to send into the abyss. May God have mercy on my soul.

For the remainder of my liberty, I stayed in my bunk, leaving only to grab some grub. Trying in vain to read one of my favorite books, one of the Sackett novels by Louis L'Amour. But my attention lay elsewhere, and the pages of the book often blurred as my mind wandered.

Conjuring up the ideal family for a child I'd never know. The father tall, strong, loving. He'd work in a bank or be a lawyer or a doctor. Someone who provided everything. Large house, fancy car, nice clothes, every toy on the market. Yet, every night, he'd make sure to take time to share the family meal and then tuck in this new child of his.

As for the mother, she'd be sweeter than pecan pie. Her whole life devoted to this new child, sunup to sundown. Giving him or her a lot of love, homemade meals, and plenty of time spent playing together. The more time I spent daydreaming, the wilder my visions of this imaginary family became.

All the while, I also drove myself mad at the thought of how lonely and sad Donna might be. Visions of her belly swelling with our child coming to me at odd times. Knowing before long she'd have to hand that child over to a set of complete strangers. All because of my act of cowardice. But undoing my actions didn't seem possible. If I ran again, I still couldn't go home. Because it'd be the first place the Army would look.

Some returned to base, others never did. None of us questioned the why of it, we understood where they'd gone. As the medic training began in May, the Texas heat became stifling. Our classrooms didn't have air conditioning. This resulted in our sleep-deprived brains finding it hard to focus on the few important nuggets in our training. No textbooks were to be had.

A few films from what appeared to be WWII formed the foundation for our medical education. Most of our instruction lay in demonstrations, then hands-on practice. No exams because, as one instructor told us, "Don't matter how bad you is, you can't fail." I wasn't sure if that sentiment was a comfort or not. Because somewhere down the line, someone would be depending on one of us to save their life.

Then again, maybe not. Much of our training looked as if it was nothing more than busy work to me. How to properly change sheets. How to fill out an FMC—Field Medical Card. How to use a bedpan. How to carry litters. That last one had to have been a joke because it came complete with an obstacle course. Up, down, weave around, jump the tires, whatever, a total waste of time as far as I was concerned.

Ten weeks filled with a bunch of nonsense.

Another graduation ceremony was soon upon me. I stood in the late July heat in the quadrangle watching the peacocks, ducks, and deer. Not wishing to look at my newly minted fellow medics at all. We were to be given two more weeks of liberty before the next step—Oakland, California, then Vietnam.

I'd sent another brief note to my mother after I'd arrived at this base to let her know I was still in Texas. Not exactly where, didn't want her to try to track me down. Also told her to not worry, I'd be a medic. Thus, I'd spend my tour healing, not killing. Not a word from me since then; I believed it to be easier on both of us somehow. I still hadn't made any decision about what to do for my last liberty. My gut told me going home remained out of the question, too many things were better if they remained unsaid.

In the end, I found a cheap motel in San Antonio for a few nights. I wandered around the Riverwalk area the next morning. Watching the ducks float lazily along, trying to find a moment of peace. Instead, I found the promenade to be crowded, noisy. It bustled with people from all walks of life and various countries of the world. Turns out San Antonio was hosting the HemisFair that summer.

Sitting beside the river, I sipped on a coffee at a small café. All the while, I'd listen to ten different languages at the same time. Swirling around me, this mashup of words from all over made me feel more confused than I already was. That first evening, I stood before the ruins of the Alamo. I stared up at this monument to courage, to men and women who took a stand for what they believed in. At that moment, I understood how much I didn't measure up.

Yes, I now held a rank in the Army, a specialized position. But that hadn't changed me, hadn't made me a better man in any way. With a heavy heart, I stumbled back to my room. As I collapsed on the edge of the bed, I stared at the pale tan walls. It'd been almost five months since I'd seen Donna. Where was she? Would it be possible to find her if I tried? Give her what pay I'd gotten up to this point? She needed the money, no way around that. But she'd sounded so sure my joining up would be the worst thing ever. Yet, in the end, what she desired most of all had been to create a family. Boy meets girl and baby makes three.

Which, because of my actions, could never be.

I flipped over onto my back, staring up at the ceiling. Everything about me felt off, wrong somehow. Giving up, I hopped off the bed. Shoved everything back into my duffle, and stormed out of the room. Ended up spending the night at the bus station, because nothing headed out in the middle of the night. Thus, I took the bus west first thing the next morning. Not caring that I'd be at my next post early.

I was ready to face Nam.

CHAPTER 7

Colorado – Present Day

"Man, I think you're being way too hard on yourself." Ryan stood, striding behind the bar where he proceeded to replenish our drinks.

I waited for him to return to his stool before choosing to add to the conversation. "Not sure how you can say that. I had, what? Four, five million opportunities to make at least a tiny gesture towards either my mother or Donna. And did I do one? No."

He took slow, measured sips, scratching his head as he did. "Look, I do believe I'd have done the same thing as you if I'd landed in the same spot. I'm almost thirty and I'm not ready to be a father. Responsibility isn't for everyone. I can't keep a spider plant alive, much less know what to do with a kid."

He chuckled. "And here's another way to look at this. If you got a girl pregnant now, everything would be different. Because single parenting isn't a big deal anymore. You were born in the wrong time, dude."

I contemplated his words for a moment. Why did everyone think I needed to be let off the hook so easily? The chaplain back in the day had tried to make me think the whole thing wasn't anything I needed to worry about. Now here Ryan was doing the same thing.

"No, what I did will always be wrong. Doesn't matter what anyone says." I chugged my new beer. The cold hit me hard, giving me a bit of a brain freeze. Plus, the buzz from all of the alcohol now had started to make me a bit numb.

"Is that why you don't want to answer this email?" His hand waved over towards the computer. "You feel you can't ever make up for abandoning her mother? You can't find a way to forgiveness?"

"In a word, yes." For the first time all day, I noticed my wedding band winking up at me. Most people were unaware of the ring's significance because I wore it on the wrong hand. Not like another option existed, I didn't have a ring finger on my left hand anymore.

I held my hand up, "See this ring? I made a vow to my wife before God to always be faithful, to grow old together, to cherish her and her alone. And I said these words less than a year after Donna told me she was carrying my child. How do I explain that? I hate myself for doing that. How can Jenny not hate me as well?"

He gnawed on his knuckles, deep in thought. "I'm now wondering something about my parents. I was born the same year my dad got back from the Gulf. But I'm not sure when my parents got married, I'm not sure I ever asked. I also don't know how they met. Well, not for sure. My mom told me something about coming in here for a bachelorette party and my dad being the bartender. My father told me he won my mom in a poker game."

He gave out a bit of a laugh at that, "While I'm sure he meant that as a joke, I do believe my mother had been the girl the bachelorette party had been thrown for. That my dad stole her from another man. Maybe my father isn't my father."

"Ryan, don't go down that rabbit hole because of my twisted life. Accept the facts your parents gave you as truth. Or better yet, ask your mother when her anniversary is."

I patted his hand, enough had been enough. We were in the weeds, it was past time for me to be moving on. "Okay, son. Thanks for the beer and for lunch. I'm heading out for greener pastures. Or at least to a bar that isn't about to come crashing down on my head." I began to rise, more than a bit unsteady on my feet.

A hand on my shoulder pushed me back down, "Oh no you don't! You can't tell me half a story and then walk out before it's finished!" He grabbed my beer, pulling it closer to him. "Plus, I do think I might have overserved you. Which is against the law. So, relax, take a load off, spin more of your yarn, and let the alcohol in your blood dilute a mite. Let me grab a few more bags of chips."

He stretched over the counter, almost falling off. Hanging upside down, wriggling as he reached far underneath. Rolling over on his back, he waved several bags high above him before he sat upright on the bar top. Dropping them near me, he hopped off onto the floor, giving me a deep bow, and returned to his seat.

"Now where were you?" He snagged a bag of chips, pulling it open with such force half of them popped out and went flying around us. "Ah, that's right. Headed off to Vietnam. Okay, continue. We'll see how sober you are after this next bit."

Pausing for a moment, I gaped at him to see how serious he might be about keeping me hostage. He munched, happy as a clam, giving me a Cheshire cat grin, not a care in the world. With my artificial hip and gimpy knee, I couldn't outrun him even if I wanted to. Not to mention the fact he'd positioned himself between me and the door. All he had to do would be to stick a leg out and trip me if I dared to move a muscle.

I picked up a snack for myself, eating a few bites as I contemplated my next move. "As I tried to explain earlier, I didn't stay in Nam for long. However, the length of my stay wasn't my problem. What I encountered there was."

CHAPTER 8

Vietnam – 1968

From basic on they called me 'College Boy.' And I do believe that's how I ended up serving in the Evac Hospital rather than being yet another grunt medic in a rice paddy.

Not like war is ever easy; my life from the moment I stepped into Vietnam became sheer torture. Didn't matter I had what most considered a cushy assignment. Three squares and a cot in the barracks, almost luxury given the situation.

At first, I tried to convince myself that my feeling the need to weep was homesickness, plain and simple. But nothing could've been further from the truth. The more things careened out of control around me, the more guilt gnawed at me for leaving Donna behind. Because by now August had arrived and with it, my child, I was sure. Yet, here in this place, I didn't want to think about something beautiful like a baby. Nothing good should, or could, come from war.

"Hey, the grub here's not that bad!" A sweet voice wafted towards me. A shadow crossed my arm as a blurry form stood beside me.

I continued to stare down at my tray, swirling my fork in the grease and slop that claimed to be my dinner. I'd been in camp a few days at this point, the noise, heat, and humidity breaking down all of my last few remaining defenses.

"I know it's hard around here at first. Scratch that—it's always impossible. You get immune to most of it eventually. By now I'm numb most of the time. Although to be fair, it's probably from the lack of sleep." She put a soft hand on my shoulder. "I'm Susan."

"Bruce," I mumbled back.

"Come on now, give me a good look. When I signed up they said this was all so 'romantic,' I'd be sure to find my husband here. Or at the very least see the world, have a grand adventure. Surely you can be a good sport and let me see your shiny mug. Then, I can figure out if you're the bloke for me or not." She let out a little giggle. "Never mind, you're just a lowly little medic. I want a doctor! And he's got to be a strapping, handsome fellow."

I did turn my head toward her at that, mostly to figure out if this was some kind of practical joke. Because who in their right mind would think of dating in a place like this? I smelled like rotting cabbage, every inch of me damp to the core. And no matter what I did I couldn't get the coppery scent of blood out of my mind, that biting acid odor lingered.

She continued to chuckle as she waltzed off, plopping beside Dr. Withers, a gent I'd been introduced to the day before.

I continued to stare at her as I mused over her words. But I couldn't quite figure out what her game was.

She'd been right about this place being impossible, however. In fact, I'd had quite a fright at the sight of some nurse barking orders to everyone. All while she stood in the middle of everything with a severed leg tucked under her arm. And that incident had happened within the first hour I'd been in the hospital for my first shift no less.

Nor did I understand how to reconcile the fact that more than a few of the patients I'd seen in the two short days I'd been here weren't soldiers. Women, children, and old people lay in the ward. This wasn't war. This looked for all the world to be a wholesale slaughter of innocents. Seems those rumors I'd heard back at Fort Sam might've had more than a bit of basis in the truth.

I hadn't even gotten through my first shift before I'd come to understand how pointless my 'training' had been. Putting in an IV for me might as well have been asking me to fly a spaceship, don't ask me what happened when I dropped one of those glass bottles. Suffice it to say all hell broke loose. You'd have thought a bomb had gone off in the middle of the ward.

I'd learned almost nothing about pharmaceutical drugs or how to dispense them. And don't get me started on how little I knew about traumatic injuries. Or what in the world I was supposed to do when I saw someone with one. These patients were dropped off by some helicopter or other and most of them looked like half a person. Missing limbs, giant holes in various places, or much worse.

I treated burn victims from white phosphorus. Many of whom had been inadequately treated in the field with copper sulfate. Thus, they'd arrive still 'on fire.' I saw napalm victims. Screams came from everyone and everywhere all at once. Yet, I couldn't close my eyes and ears to shut out the chaos.

No, I had a job to do, no matter how difficult it may be. I had to care for my fellow man. No matter what condition they may arrive in, half-alive or mostly dead, the job remained the same: patch them up, fast. Which left my soul in shreds in a matter of moments on my first day.

One thing from my civilian life remained, which did come in handy amid the chaos. My pocket knife. I'd use it to remove boots, bits of clothing, whatever. Because as I discovered rather quickly, I'd rather carry that knife in my pocket than a pair of scissors.

Plus, during off hours, I'd use it to take my mind off things and whittle. Make little shapes out of scraps of wood, bears, cows, or the like. I'd bring these into the ward for the kids. Not a real toy, but something for them to hold onto. Something to ease their minds, to keep them from thinking about the pain. Or this damn war.

The other guys in the barracks drank heavily to ease their consciousnesses or simply to be able to sleep. In the beginning, I waved off the many offers of beer. Instead, I'd flip through the booklet I'd been given—The Combat Medic. A rather basic little leaflet with information about what my job entailed and what the Army expected of me. The language in the stupid thing was simple and borderline patronizing.

One line I loved best. Under the part about what I'd been trained to do: 'Request assistance when the case is bigger than you can handle.' Every case I'd seen fell into this category. However, to me, the logical and reasonable move wasn't to turn to anyone for help. Not with everyone else running around, in full crisis mode most of the time.

Plus, a whole section spoke about all of the paperwork I had to do. And a snarky statement about 'never let the paperwork interfere with the care of the patient.' Again, if I didn't fill out the damn paperwork, then I couldn't ask for assistance. Giving me the sense I'd landed on some Army hamster wheel with no way off.

By the end of my first week, I had to admit I couldn't deal with Nam sober. I need something to numb me, to take the edge off. I gulped that lukewarm beer and then grabbed another.

My mind replayed the scene from earlier in the day when I'd held a dying man in my arms. The whole time he'd screamed in pain, and for his mother. And I hadn't been able to do anything to make things better. He'd lost both his legs, half his insides. Don't ask me how they'd managed to get him to us on a stretcher, not in a body bag. We were so far behind the frontlines.

"Hey College Boy, slow down! Save some for the rest of us." Chuck laughed as he reclined on his bunk, flipping through the latest nudie magazine he'd found. Wearing only his boxers, his ebony skin glistened with sweat.

Despite the fact it was now near midnight, the temps hovered around eighty with one hundred percent humidity.

"How does anyone handle this?" I wiped my mouth with the back of my hand, cradling the foul brew in the other.

"Getting drunk every night helps. Going to the beach when we can. Finding a local girl to cuddle up with does wonders." Jorge called out from his bunk in the corner.

Well, out of the three, getting drunk seemed to be the quickest and most reasonable solution.

My workday saw a variety of things to deal with. Trauma of the worst kind. Snakebites, scorpion bites, centipede or millipede bites, rat bites, fire ant bites, leeches. Lacerations from barbed wire. Skin problems from infections, fungus, jungle rot, boils, trench foot. Eye injuries from all manner of things. And of course, the ever-present problems of heat exhaustion and various tropical diseases.

One of the doctors with whom I worked had trained as a gynecologist. Yet, here he was supposed to be helping me treat patients from this war. Lucky for me he recognized his limits. He understood when to call for backup from another doctor with a greater skillset in trauma. And he also knew to give credit when credit was due.

I overheard him tell a new doctor, "If you have any trouble treating skin diseases, ask the medics who've been here a while. If they can't cure it, you probably won't be able to affect a cure either. Don't be afraid to consult with them."

That new doctor gazed over at us medics with a rather skeptical look, his eyebrows drawn down, a frown on his face. "They didn't go to medical school. I'd rather not discuss treatment options with them."

But that guy didn't know what he was up against yet. I'd been in Nam a few weeks at that point and I already had learned more than I'd ever wanted to. I figured he'd get with the program soon enough, find out what we already knew: That when you thought you'd seen the worst, wait five minutes.

Many of the medics had the time and patience to consult with the locals. Which is how they came to know so much about local cures. Herbs and things that worked better than anything the Army passed out. Our Western medicine wasn't any match for some of the crazy stuff we encountered on a given day.

Susan and I often had the same duty shift; we'd work side by side on the same wounded patient. Soldier or local, didn't matter, blood was blood. On our breaks, we would chit-chat sometimes as we'd pass cigarettes. We'd stand just past the back door of the hospital, easy access to the ward just in case we'd get called back.

She'd volunteered for the Red Cross to try to find her brother. No letters had come after he'd been drafted and sent off. Ended up in Nam as an Army nurse. I hesitated to tell her of my own failure at contacting family as well. Seeing the pain on her face as she talked about her brother only served to remind me of my mother.

"Do you ever wonder why we're here?" She asked me one night.

"We signed on the dotted line," I responded, unsure what she meant. We'd both come by choice not because someone told us we had to. A common bond we shared, one of the few.

"No, I mean, the real reason behind the war." She glanced over at me, tears in her eyes. "We're seeing too many men who are harming themselves. They shoot their toes off. They drop something heavy like an ammo box or a mortar crate on their arm or leg. They set off a trip flare while holding it. They know this war is wrong. They know there's so much meaningless death of good people and no one can stop it."

"I don't know, I don't think anyone knows." I dropped the butt, grinding it beneath my heel.

"I had this patient today, he claimed that the Geneva Convention wasn't being respected by either side. That there's no good guy in this fight." She placed a small hand on my arm, so much pain written on her face.

The same sentiment as had been shared back in basic: we may be the bad guys, not the good guys. That we hadn't come here to be the white knights who save everyone from evil. I reached over to rub her back, then moved up to her hair, pulling her towards me. At that moment I needed her, and I started to lean in to kiss her. But she recoiled from my overtures, taking more than a few steps back.

"I'm sorry." Pushing off from the wall, I stalked back into the ward.

Resumed my work as if nothing had happened between us.

Many nights, our enemy, whom we nicknamed Charlie, had a nasty habit of raining mortars down on us. Sneaking out of the jungle, enemy troops appeared long enough to harass us before vanishing back into the night. Their sole intent to try to keep us awake, off guard, unprepared. As if everything else around us wasn't enough to demoralize us, we got so little sleep on top of everything else. One moment, my eyes would flutter at an attempt at rest. The next I'd be running for my life. Each moment on base worse than the last.

I ended up moving like a sleepwalker, not awake but not asleep. Doing my job, returning to the barracks to get drunk, repeat the next day. My uniform hung off me as I dropped weight like I was shedding what remained of my old life. And this position I'd landed in most considered good, one of the best in Nam. But here I was, falling to pieces, unable to cope.

Often flashes of Donna and our weekend together would pop into my mind. Usually after I'd had more than a few too many beers. I would feel her skin against mine, the flavor of the cherry lip balm on her lips. And wish for that moment again.

But it could never be.

Then, the day came when my life took another turn sideways. I crossed the yard one afternoon at the end of yet another long shift. All my thoughts were on my cot and the booze hidden beneath it. Nothing else mattered anymore.

"Hey, Johnson! The medic from the Dust Off that just arrived needs to be relieved. Hop on for the next flight!" A sergeant I hardly knew yelled at me.

I wanted to say 'no,' but that's not an option in this man's army.

So off I went, not a word of complaint, not a grunt of dissatisfaction about the inconvenience of it all. My sole hope I tried to latch onto was this might be a temporary situation. That the other medic might not be seriously wounded, or in fact, might not be harmed at all. Maybe he had a rash, something minor and my assignment to the Dust Off team would be a one-and-done thing.

The noise from the blades hurt my ears, the chopper flew so low to the ground, it left me afraid we'd hit a tree or a house. During the flight, I did little more than stare at the corpsman across from me. Dirty, lined face bearing the weight of the world. Despite the fact he couldn't be any older than me, his eyes were dark hollows. He'd seen more than any boy should at this point. We all had, didn't matter what our post might be.

He seemed familiar, I knew him from somewhere, not just the base. But I couldn't put my finger on why. It might have been nothing more than all of us were the same. We dressed alike, we sounded alike, we looked alike. This man replaces that, nobody notices or cares.

Green as far as the eye can see.

We landed, I jumped off and rushed to those who waved at me. The corpsman at my heel, "Hustle, man, hustle!"

"Give me time, I've got to assess the patient!" I threw over my shoulder.

"Not your job. Scoop and run, man." He pushed my shoulder hard.

Then all hell broke loose, shelling from everywhere and nowhere. The ground beneath me shook, as each bomb landed. The din around me made it impossible to hear what everyone around me was yelling. Their lips moved but no human sound would ever be loud enough to overcome the shock of the mortars. This area not being anywhere I'd been before, I scrambled. Sliding and slipping through the mud, I tried in vain to follow the soldiers around me to the nearest place of safety. And I failed, by a few seconds. My left hand had been on the edge of the hole I'd dove into at the time of the blast.

My last memory of that moment would be forever seared in my brain. The corpsman from the chopper I'd been on had been even less successful than I'd been. He'd been right behind me, and he didn't end up in that hole by choice. He'd been thrown in by the force of an explosion. His body ripped to shreds, landing on top of me. I'd ended up covered in what little remained of him. Blood, gore, his shocked face staring into mine.

As for me, a slight concussion, a few broken ribs, bits of debris in my left arm and side. I'd been told I'd been damn lucky to get to keep any of my fingers. How I managed to end back where I'd started remained nothing more than a guess. One moment, I closed my eyes at the sight of destruction and the next I gazed up at Susan.

I lay in a bed in the same damn hospital I'd formerly worked in. I'd been placed in a far corner, given as much privacy as possible given the situation. But everything hummed and bustled around me. Wounded patients were moved in and out. Others were tended to, injuries bandaged or casts adjusted. Others doing my job while I remained helpless. One arm propped on a hard pillow, my hand invisible in its soft cocoon. My side wrapped with gauze, my head splitting with the mother of all headaches.

Susan fussed over me often, "Now, do you need anything? More pain meds? Your pillows adjusted? Me to pray with you?"

No, no, no, and no. Leave me the hell alone. But I couldn't say that to her kind face.

Instead, I remained in silence. Trying to give her a hint of a smile. All while flashes of that corpsman filled my mind. It's not like we were buddies, mates, friends. Yes, I'd seen him around. I'd helped to move patients from the landing area to the hospital on more than one occasion after all. And one mess hall fed the lot of us. But still, I didn't even know his name until now. I overheard someone talking about what a great guy Corpsman Richards had been. And they mentioned that he'd come from Kansas, a farm kid like me.

We had a lot in common, we could've been mates. But, no. I'd said 'Hi,' or 'How's it going today?' a few times. More often than not, we'd just give each other nods. We floated in the same orbit by the nature of our respective jobs, nothing more. And now he'd become compost, forever part of the soil of this foreign land.

But the stain of his blood I couldn't get off, didn't matter how many times Susan washed my skin. All of my body sticky and wet; to me, my skin appeared stained a dark red. That man would be with me for the rest of my life. My buddies brought me beer, it didn't matter to me it wouldn't mix well with the pain meds. This I needed more than anything else.

Susan stopped by. "It'd be best if you talk about what happened."

"Nothing to talk about. I got knocked out before I saw anything." I turned my head to look at the wall.

Inside I believed nothing would bring me back to life. Not after this.

"They say you've got your ticket home, Bruce," Susan adjusted the bandages on my hand and arm. "That's a good thing, right? You won't have to see any of this ever again."

"Come with me, you don't have to stay here. We could do something better, go anywhere. Take off from here. Forget America, forget everything. There's a whole world waiting for us. How much of it have you seen? All I've seen is my home state and this fudging mess." I reached over with my good hand, pulling her against me in my bed. Not caring that the action caused shooting pain in my side.

She stared deep into my eyes for a moment, then pushed off me. Rising, she adjusted her uniform, glancing this way and that. "You know it'd never work. We aren't meant to be. I'm sorry, Bruce." And she stalked off to tend to someone else.

Over the course of the next day or so, the warmth between us had turned to an arctic frost. She often had someone else assist me. Often not even giving me one glance as she paced the ward while she performed her duties.

In the end, on the day I walked out of the ward for good, I switched from pajamas to my uniform once again. She walked my way, giving me a sad smile.

I tugged on the lapel of my jacket, wishing more than anything to avoid looking at her, speaking to her, or saying goodbye. Trying to keep my coat in place with only one arm in a sleeve, I failed. It kept getting hung up on my sling and she reached over to tuck it in place.

"Live a good life, Bruce. Go find what you're looking for." She gave me a quick peck on the cheek, a soft squeeze on my shoulder. "Be happy."

"No point in that. I've been a fool." Spinning, I began to march towards the door. "I'll never find peace again."

"No." She called out to my retreating back. "You have so much more to give. Don't ever give up on yourself!"

But I didn't turn around or respond in any way. Nothing lived in my soul anymore. I knew she was wrong. I had nothing left to give. Not to her, not to anyone. I left Nam nothing more than an empty shell.

CHAPTER 9

Colorado – Present Day

It amazed me how much I remembered from my short time in Nam. Those little details didn't fade with time. Nor did the pain I once endured from a war long over. Not only the agony of my physical wounds but the mental and mortal ones as well.

Because no matter what I did I couldn't forget any of it even if I wanted to.

Nam is what I awakened to almost every morning when I stepped out of bed. It's what haunted my dreams so often even after all of these years. But it's now a memory I choose to grow from, not be engulfed by. After all, life is change, growth is optional. By the grace of God, I'd learned to choose with a bit more wisdom over the years.

I gave the odd-shaped side of my hand a gentle rub. This constant reminder that every day I lived was both a blessing and a curse. "See, a few weeks in war doesn't give me the right to be anything less than a coward. I couldn't even figure out how to get my butt into a foxhole properly."

"I'm thinking your reactions to everything has more to do with what you saw than what happened to you. Did you really see all of those injured children?" Ryan grimaced, pain on his face.

"Yes. Horrible injuries, burns, gunshots, shrapnel from goodness only knows what. I'm not sure how Vietnam endured as a country with all of those innocents getting slaughtered the way they did. How did enough people survive to produce the next generation? But I guess humans always find a way to carry on, no matter how great of a cost it may be."

I tried my best to wipe the images from my mind. Those children, so malnourished, so small, so frail. Destroyed by everyone, everything, with no way to protect themselves.

"And that's why you came home different. You'd seen the worst of humanity. You'd seen someone die right in front of you. But why not go back and find your girl?" His question reasonable on its face, but he didn't understand the place I'd been in at the time. "There must have been some kernel of love left inside of you, despite everything."

"I'd come home damaged in so many ways. I couldn't face myself. How would I be able to face Donna and our child?" Those nightmares from Nam are my ever-present companions, although not as often as they once were to be sure. Yet, even now, I wake drenched in sweat on more than a few nights, filled with panic. All over something that happened to a man I used to be in a different life.

"I'm not the right guy to ask that question of. I didn't have anything major happen to me and I can't reply to even a simple text from my girl anymore." Ryan chuckled, giving a slight shake of his head. "Then again, it's not like she's planted in Florida. She could've followed me here. Come to think of it, why didn't she? Why is she expecting me to make all the changes? Never mind, I guess that one's on me for not having a straight conversation with her at some point."

"Son, do you regret leaving her? Do you ache at the thought you don't see her every day?" I stared at him, watching as his eyes widened then narrowed as he pondered my questions.

"No. For the first time in years, I'm breathing without needing permission." He waved a hand around the room. "There's something freeing about doing whatever the heck you want and not giving a darn who doesn't approve."

"Then call her, tell her it's officially over. And do what you need to do for you. Stop using this dump as an excuse to not move forward."

The kick in the rear he needed, and something I needed to hear as well. Because by this point, even I saw that I was stalling. Talking about everything in the past didn't change the fact I had to respond to the email. But the second I did, the world I'd created would end. If it hadn't already. Would I ever be ready for that?

"Hey, little harsh there! I love this bar! With a little work, it'd be possible to bring this place back to its old charm." He gave me his best smile, patting hard on the stool next to him as he did.

The stool wobbled for a moment, one leg crumbled and the thing crashed to the floor. The sound rang out in the empty room, loud and unforgiving in the ensuing silence. Ryan began to laugh, tears streaming down his face as he did.

"Sure, a wrecking ball wouldn't hurt!" He howled, clutching the side of the counter. "Start over from scratch and turn this into something a bit more modern, say from the thirties!"

Shifting a bit, I glanced down at the remnants of the stool. How easy it is for things to fall apart, be left by the wayside. A moment of carelessness, a moment of weakness, and a mess is left in our wake.

I'd always left those disasters in my rearview, not wishing to clean up after myself. Until now. The room grew quiet again, yet I continued to stare at the floor.

A hand waved in front of my face, "Hey, earth to Bruce. You okay?"

I swiped a hand over my eyes, trying to make my vision less blurry. I shifted my gaze back up to him. "Sure, just not used to knocking back a few so early in the day is all."

"Guess the chips weren't enough. Want another sandwich?" He started to rise, I patted his shoulder to stop him.

He'd believed my slight stretching of the truth, however, I was angry at myself for not being honest with him. "Won't help." I tipped my head up to take another long look at the ceiling. "I need to take my own advice. Tell this new daughter of mine what she wants to hear."

"And what do you think that is?" His voice seemed to come to me in an echo.

"I sure wish I knew what in the hell that was." I rose, stretched, took a few steps towards the door. Then paced toward the far wall, finally finishing the circuit back at my seat. "How do I explain to her that I've been pretending for years that she didn't even exist?" I started to crack my knuckles, satisfied with the sound of each pop.

"Is that really what you did?" He swiped at the counter with his hand, sending a few stray crumbs off into the unknown. Adding to the grime already on the floor, dirt held this place together. Nothing more, nothing less.

"Yes. My wife Nancy believes she was my first girl." So much easier for a man to pull that one off than a woman. "I've never acknowledged what I left behind in Texas. Until now. Back then a way to find me didn't exist. No internet making it impossible to hide. No DNA tests to take. Everything is so much more complicated now."

He squeezed my hand in a firm grip, "But all of those things have been around for quite a while. The thought that your child might be looking for you had to have crossed your mind at some point, yes?"

Gulping hard, I looked down at my worn boots. "Sure, but when is the right time to come out from the rock you've been hiding under? Ten years? Twenty? Fifty?" I grasped his hand tight, with as much pressure as I felt safe to do. "And what do you tell all of those people you've been lying to when you do?"

"Ah, now who've you been lying to? You seem like a rather straight-up guy. Despite having made some rather questionable decisions in life, I'd trust you." He looked deep into my eyes, trying to read me on a level I wasn't comfortable with.

Because here is where the tale takes a turn. Ryan had been with me up to this point, however, I rather doubted this would still be the case if I continued on. "Look, my life's a twisted path leading to nowhere but here, this moment with you. One in which I'm running from both my wife and my child. Everyone deserves a few answers, and nobody's gonna like them."

"Are you running or are you trying to get your mind straight as to how best not to let everyone down?" He frowned, "Because, again, this is how I'm reading the situation. You give the impression you put too much pressure on yourself to do what everyone wants you to do. Have you considered those answers you're having problems spitting out might make things better? Not worse? Because maybe things will make more sense to those around you now that everything is out in the open?"

Not sure how much better things would be. I'd gotten rather comfortable with the status quo. I'd learned to roll with things rather than fight against them. "That might be the case for Jenny but I rather doubt it will be for Nancy. Our whole marriage was based on a lie."

CHAPTER 10

California and Colorado – 1968

After those few days of treatment, it turned out to be true. Losing a few fingers was enough to be shipped stateside. Got myself orders to be sent from Vietnam to a base in San Francisco, California to recover from my wounds. Plus, I'd need a second surgery on my hand. I'd also been told I'd more than likely have to spend the rest of my hitch doing grunt work at the hospital. Not something I looked forward to doing in the least.

This flight wasn't the same as the first. Instead of the midpoint being Alaska, we stopped to refuel in Japan. Now I'd be able to boast I'd been to two foreign countries. Sure, the stop had only been for a few hours and I never got out of the airport. But goody for me for being such a world traveler. However, my mind couldn't process anything. Everywhere I looked, all I saw were flashes of those pieces of the corpsman who'd landed on me. The metallic odor of his blood filled my nostrils; I felt the weight of his body on my skin. I couldn't escape.

Because I'd been declared 'walking wounded,' I stepped off the plane in San Francisco, along with the able-bodied who'd finished their year-long tours. Into a world of hate. We were marched along the perimeter fence, on the other side a sea of protesters. Men, women, hippies one and all. Signs declaring us 'baby killers' along with others bearing the words like 'make love, not war.' They screamed at the top of their lungs, they spat on us. They chanted and banged on things or rattled the links of the fence.

I cried in my heart as I marched past, silent with no tears, my head hung in shame. I hadn't killed anyone. I hadn't even touched a weapon my entire time in country. My job had been to treat the suffering, the dying. To be a healer, confidant, friend, counselor to my brothers-in-arms. And I'd paid dearly for my service. Yet, here in my home country, I'd now become the enemy.

In a cavernous building, a man gave me the once over, handing me my orders for the next stage of my journey. I shuffled along, going to the place I'd been told to go. My duffel on my back, my mind reeling from the 'welcome' I'd received. I didn't bother to glance out at the streets of the city we drove through, no point in that. I didn't belong here, I no longer belonged anywhere.

The hospital I was dropped off at didn't make me feel any better. From the first moment I arrived, my gut told me I'd last two days tops. An orderly showed me to my assigned bed in a ward for those like me. Standing still for a moment, I scanned the area.

The patients around me were a sad reminder of the mess and destruction of the war I'd left behind. Men so mangled in mind, body, and spirit, they were hard to be around. Groans came from every bed in the room. Missing limbs on almost everyone I spotted. Eyes glazed, staring into nothing.

These men had seen combat, unlike me, and appeared to still be wrestling with the aftermath. I hesitated for a moment, still unwilling to sit on my bed. These men were me. And my heart screamed at me that if I remained here, I'd end up in the same wretched state as them.

"Mr. Johnson, I see here you're scheduled for a flap repair on your hand. Plus, we need to check to ensure that all the shrapnel has been removed from your arm and side." A nurse had come up behind me, causing me to jump to one side.

Giving my heartbeat a moment to slow down again, I stared at her. Plump, older, with more wrinkles than skin on her frowning face. Her grey hair escaped out from underneath her white cap. Her white uniform strained against her many bulges, her ankles rolled over the tops of her shoes. Her fat fingers flipped through the paperwork I'd shown up with. She didn't even give me a sideways glance.

"Yes ma'am." I placed my duffle on the bed, taking another step away from this dreadful woman. Something about her grated on me, nothing about her appeared to be warm or tender. How she'd ended up here, I didn't have a clue.

"I'll go get your medication while you get settled." She patted the thin cover on the bed as she spun on the heels of her stained white shoes, causing them to squeak.

As I watched her retreating back, I knew I couldn't wait for her to return. Grabbing my stuff again, I left the hospital not caring that no one had given me permission to or not. Didn't feel my 'injury' measured up to all the fussing those others were clearly in need of.

A few fingers missing being a rather minor thing and all. And I didn't care to serve the army for one second more. Nor did I care if someone came after me later, as far as I was concerned going AWOL had become a necessity to save my sanity. And my mental health had to be my top priority right at that moment.

But where I wanted to be instead, turned out to be a whole other kettle of fish. The way I looked marked me as a soldier, I needed to not have short hair. My hand needed to finish healing with or without additional medical intervention. And my straight back needed to loosen.

No, I don't think becoming a hippy had been my goal exactly. Or, in fact, had even crossed my mind. Just needed to better blend in to the landscape so no one would ask if I'd been to Nam. I didn't want to be peppered with questions about where I'd come from. What I'd witnessed had to be left buried in the past.

One thing I did know—I couldn't face my mother. Not yet. Not only because it'd be the first place the Army would try to find me, if they should decide I was worth looking for. Given the rumors I'd heard about deserters, I kinda doubted I'd be on anyone's radar. Too many others had done the same thing.

But the fact remained: my mother didn't need me to come home a shattered shell. I figured I'd show up sooner or later when I had found a way to return to my former confident, boyhood self. When I wouldn't be likely to cry and spill out everything I'd kept hidden.

But was it even possible to become the person I used to be, erase the last year or so from my life as if it'd never happened? Prayer and going to church had gone out the window. So many other things had as well during those few months I'd been at college. Wasn't sure if my problems had started because of that small act, or if they had already begun by then. But Susan telling me to pray after I'd been injured had reminded me of my mother. And how some believed this God might be a rock to cling to during the hard times. Yet, from what I had seen, He hadn't done much for my mother in all those years of her serving faithfully in the church. Why did I expect Him to do anything for me?

I'd been smart and had most of my pay deposited into my Bank of America account. My thought had been to save the money for Donna and the baby, irrational as that might have been. Yet, now that I'd turned my back on the Army, I needed money in the worst way. Closing out the account that day wasn't a problem, the woman at the bank didn't even blink when I made the request. My next thought as I exited the bank: I needed wheels. Walking would get me nowhere fast.

Buying a beat-up old Ford truck from a small dealership, a wave of nostalgia washed over me. Flooded with happiness and memories of better times, warmth filled every inch of me for a second. This truck and the old one from the farm were almost identical, one blue, the other green. Both dented, scarred, used for all kinds of work. The vinyl bench seats cracked and faded; the dash spotted by the sun. As an added plus, it'd been the cheapest thing on the lot.

A few hours after I'd arrived in San Francisco, I hit the road. My plan a rather simple one: find a place to lay low until I could think of what to do with the rest of my life. My skillset of various trades learned on the farm would always lead to work, hard labor no stranger to me. Yet deep down I had no desire to go back to that life or anything even close to it. My heart might want me to go home but my head kept telling me the truth. You can't ever go home again. Some roads can't be taken twice.

Nor should they be.

Finding little camping spots along the backroads in California, I wandered for days, weeks. Slapping up a personal tent I'd gotten for days when the weather might be foul. Sleeping in the bed of the truck on nights when it wasn't. I preferred being out in the open, staring at the twinkling stars, since sleep often eluded me anyway.

I fished for my dinner most days, relaxing under the early fall sun as I waited for a bite on the end of my rod. Pretending that by now Donna hadn't given birth to our child somewhere. That our child wasn't nestled right now in the arms of strangers.

Also, I ignored the fact that my family would be wondering where I'd disappeared to. Because I didn't send anything more than a single note on my first day back in the States. A quick little postcard from San Francisco that I'd picked up. I'd filled out and mailed it at the gas station on my way out of town. But when one is AWOL, one can't go announcing to one and all their every move.

Peace came to me in waves. Some days I'd be fine with the world, others I'd cry from sunup to sundown. Here I was, a grown man who had gone to war and had a baby out there somewhere more than likely. Yet somehow, I couldn't find a way to get a handle on my emotions, my thoughts, my memories.

Visions of torn bodies lying in their beds in the wards or in the triage area flooded my dreams. That is on those nights I'd manage to get a wink or two in. And that moment with the corpsman often would play on repeat, looped again and again. A whole man standing right over me, a man torn asunder all over me. No way to ever erase that image.

I ended up drowning myself in more than a drop or two of whiskey in order to achieve those precious moments of sleep. I started with beer and worked my way up. Nothing else worked, even the whiskey didn't most of the time. No matter how tired I became because of physical exertion, sleeping became an impossibility most nights. Nightmares became my constant nemesis.

It didn't matter how many times I tried to remind myself that I'd been the lucky one. That I'd walked away almost unscathed. I'd seen the horrors of war, the carnage done to humans. The body of Corpsman Richards that'd landed on top of me in the foxhole hadn't gotten off easy. Nor had all of those mangled children in the evac wards.

My gut told me it'd been best I'd been shipped back so soon after my arrival. I'd have gone crazy for sure seeing much more of that bloodshed. Hard to believe I'd arrived in Vietnam at the start of August and now here I was in late October, in the middle of nowhere. So much hardship crammed into less than two months in some distant country. I'd been back almost the same amount of time and still hadn't been able to move past it. At this rate, I never would.

As I turned scruffier, I headed the nose of my truck toward Nevada. I'd burned all my Army gear by now, tossing piece by piece into various campfires. Nothing left that might mark me as a former soldier. I kept one thing from my former life—my pocket knife. Something inside told me to hang on to this sole memento. Sure, it'd be easy enough to buy another one. No reason at all to keep it. But rubbing it as I put a hand in my pocket brought a spark of calm to my troubled soul. A talisman against evil.

Winter would soon be upon me. I found a cheap motel to hole up in for a while. But being inside a building again suffocated me, to the point of it being painful. I found a place to buy an inexpensive camper topper for my truck. Nothing fancy, the bare bones model, and used at that. Basic shelter, a place to lay my head when the need might arise. Or to sit in when it rained, reading my favorite Sackett novel I'd found at a thrift store. Trying in vain to regain some semblance of normalcy in my life.

By now, I'd grown a scraggly beard, my hair hitting close to my collar. My clothes were all rags from some second-hand shops I'd found along the way. My bit of pay from the war wasn't going to hold out forever—I'd have to find work sooner rather than later. However, who'd hire this bum? I'd gone from somewhat respectable small-town college boy to war medic to homeless in less than a year. And lost everything I had been along the way.

Leaving Nevada in my rearview, I headed north, winding my way through the Rockies in Utah. Snow fell soft around me most days. I ended up with a big ol' pile of blankets and sleeping bags on top of my thin mattress to keep me warm. Yes, my topper had a heater built in as well as a stovetop for me to cook with. Both of which I had more than a bit of reluctance to use. For reasons I couldn't explain, the pungent odor of gas nauseated me.

Continuing on a path to nowhere, I found myself in a little town in Colorado. Facing the onslaught of a massive storm bearing down on the area, I'd gotten stuck. I hadn't had enough time to find an out-of-the-way spot to hide myself from the world. The small state-run campground next to the ski hill would have to do for the duration. After setting up my truck in the assigned space, I headed out.

As I hiked through the swirling drifts, the bitter wind bit my exposed cheeks. Heading off, I tried to find the local watering hole the camp host had told me was nearby. Regretting I hadn't spotted a liquor store all day and I'd already drunk my last drop the day before.

Yanking open the heavy wooden door, warmth blasted me. Inside, the bright, welcoming room called to me. But to my horror, people packed every inch of the place, the twang of country music blaring from somewhere. My hand released the brass handle as my body did a slow pivot and I turned to leave.

People and I weren't meant to be in the same space, not anymore. A tug on my coat as fingers pulled my arm toward them. I rotated my head to see who the intruder might be. A face swallowed up in a fur-lined hood smiled back at me. Eyes twinkled at me from beneath whispers of soft brown bangs.

"It's better inside, out here you might freeze to death in a few seconds." She giggled as she reached a mittened hand out to swipe a flake or two off the tip of my nose. She moved closer to the door, never letting go of my sleeve. "Come on now, hurry up before we turn into two popsicles!"

The idea of somewhere comfortable, cozy, snug, tugged at my soul. Even if for only long enough to slug down a shot or two to numb my senses for the remainder of the night. Made me feel almost human in a way nothing else had in a very long time. I shifted my weight, taking one slow step inside the small entry. A hall lined with coats, scarves, and other paraphernalia shed as others had made their way out of the storm.

She peeled off several heavy layers, revealing a chunky sweater, knitted in a bold orange, red, yellow, and navy pattern of waves and swirls. This she'd worn over a pair of worn bell-bottomed jeans. I didn't have layers on. Thus, I merely undid the zipper part way down on my jacket which was much too thin for this type of weather.

We strolled over to the bar, she shoved another patron off a worn stool, giving it a slap with her hand after she had. "Best seat in the house for our newest guest." She tilted her head up to me with a smile. Looking to either side, I wondered where she planned to park herself— no other stools were empty.

Without another word, she waltzed behind the bar. She proceeded to snag a crisp, clean apron from a hook hanging on the wall and donned it upon her thick waist. "So, what'll it be?" She tapped on my meaty paw still encased in its leather work glove.

"A shot of your strongest stuff." Taking off my gloves, I slipped them into a pocket. Doing my best to keep my mangled hand out of sight in my lap, I tapped on the counter with the fingers of the other hand.

She gave me a good hard stare, pursing her lips before frowning slightly. "No, you can't be that cold. And even though you look like a hippy, you don't carry yourself that way. Just back from Nam? Trying to drown your sorrows?"

Gulping at her directness, I began to rise from my chair. Certain things I no longer discussed, things in my life that needed to be kept away from prying eyes. "No. Never mind the drink." In my haste, the not quite healed edge of my hand hit the side of the counter causing me to emit a loud groan. In agony at the white-hot pain racing up my arm, I sank back down.

"Sure." She turned, busying herself for a moment with getting me a glass of something. "This will fix you right up."

Grabbing the large glass, I swallowed most of the amber liquid in one quick swig. Coughing as the foul hint of mud and ginger hit the back of my throat, "What the...?"

"Moonshine. Best stuff in the joint." She giggled. "So, Mr. I'm Fine and Dandy. You must be here for the great skiing. With all this new snow, the powder's going to be great tomorrow. Hope your skis are waxed and ready!"

"Nancy!" At this she turned her head toward another man, then returned her gaze back to me. She gave me a nod before scooting off down the bar to tend to other patrons.

I glanced around in silence for a few moments, wondering what I should do next. My head yelled at me to get out while the getting was good. Yet some part of me was wondering how this woman had figured out so much about me in a mere few seconds. In the end, the warmth of both the drink and the bar filled me and my butt remained planted in its seat. My eyes focused on Nancy alone, and the rest of the room blurred.

Her small frame sturdy and stout. What we in Texas call 'farm girl cute.' Long, thin face with a narrow nose. Dark brown oval eyes, which danced in delight at everything. Her long, dark brown hair she'd pulled back into a loose ponytail that bobbed as she waltzed around the room.

I tuned out the noise swirling around me, picturing what it would be like to go for a walk with this woman. Something simple like that first night with Donna. Was that even something I was capable of doing anymore?

I'd turned into something of a hermit, content to remain buried deep in my shell. Concealed from the world, unable to harm others or be harmed again. However, the nightmares invaded, over and over again. They stood as a constant reminder that I'd never be safe, whole, normal.

No girl in her right mind would ever want me, damaged, flawed, scarred as I now had become. Not my hand, hiding that had become second nature. As I'd done with the glove, by stuffing the empty fingers with cotton. No, my heart, soul, mind. Those parts of me not only couldn't be kept from prying eyes, but I also couldn't fix them.

After a bit, Nancy wandered back toward me and I motioned to my glass to indicate I wanted another. She shook her head 'No,' frowning as she did so. Her liquid chocolate eyes wide, her nostrils flared. Her finger gave me a little waggle of disapproval.

She resumed her work and went out into the crowded room laden with a tray of drinks. Spotting an older gent pulling a beer, I figured my best move was to get service from someone else. A place this busy had to be crawling with staff, so Nancy could take her attitude elsewhere. When he had finished his task, I banged my glass on the countertop, begging for attention. He looked my way for a moment, squinting his eyes at me, making me feel quite small.

I'm the customer here. "Hey, I need a drink!" I yelled over the din, leaning over the bar as I did.

The customer next to me shoved me back down into my seat, I elbowed him back. He stood up, legs straddled, winding up to take a swing. Then he wobbled for a moment before falling on his ass.

The man behind the bar approached, snatching up our empty glasses. "You two clowns have had enough. You're welcome to continue to enjoy the atmosphere but I'm not tolerating no drunks."

A few other patrons helped their compadre off the floor, dusting him off before planting him in a chair on the other side of the room.

One drink. One lousy drink had been all I got and it wasn't enough to even give me more than a slight buzz. It's for darn sure that it didn't make the world even a tiny bit better. Standing, I hauled my gloves back out of my pocket, sliding them on with haste. As I began my retreat back out the door, a hand pulled on my arm.

"We haven't finished our date yet, don't walk out on me so soon." A sweet voice whispered in my ear, the cloying aroma of jasmine wafting around me. "You haven't even told me your name, my dear boy."

As I turned my head to look into her eyes, something inside of me broke. The waft of her perfume filled every inch of me, overpowering me. The burden I carried had to be shared, the load couldn't be shouldered alone any longer. Tears began a slow crawl down my cheeks. No words existed to express the emotions racing within me and I'm not sure she'd have understood even if I'd said anything anyway.

She dropped her now empty tray on a table with a loud clank, guiding me toward the back. "Henry, I'm done for the night." She called out over her shoulder, to whom I wasn't sure. Not like I cared one iota at that point.

Continuing to follow her lead, we went into the dark recesses of a hallway, up a set of stairs, ending in a large office. Settling onto a large black leather sofa, she nestled me into her arms. Allowing me the space I needed to start spinning my web of lies. All because I didn't know how to tell anyone the truth. I'd never been anywhere, I'd always lived nearby, my hand my own damn fault, I'd just learned my old buddy had been killed. On and on I went, once I'd stopped blubbering on her ample chest.

CHAPTER 11

Colorado – Present Day

"Seriously, from day one you lied to your wife?" Ryan's fist bumped his mouth, trying to cover those words he'd uttered. All to pretend he hadn't been that upfront with his question.

Yup, no way to get around that one, however. This fact haunted me from that night on. Nancy wanted nothing more than to help ease whatever troubled me, whatever gnawed at my soul. And I, unable and unwilling to let the real truth come out, spilled my guts without revealing anything important.

Because it'd been a pack of lies, nothing honest about it. To be fair, a grain of truth lay in some of what I shared. For a brief moment, a tiny instant, I'd considered being upfront. But something deep within held me back, told me she'd throw me out into the snow if I did. But at that instant, I needed a connection. In that bar, I could see I'd been slowly killing myself for months. She alone held my one shot at returning to some sort of normal. However, my life up to that point held too many moments I couldn't handle. There wasn't any way I could place all of my burdens upon another.

"Not exactly. I did mention something about a buddy of mine getting killed in Nam. Well, sure, I didn't even know that corpsman's name until after his death. And, okay, I also didn't mention he'd died in front of me. But my feelings of survivor's guilt were very real either way." I swallowed hard.

How could I still be trying to justify my actions? I deflated like a balloon, my real self nothing more than a fraud, an idiot, a failure. Again.

"What did you say about that?" He gestured to my damaged hand, "I mean, it's not like you can hide that from anyone. Almost half your hand is gone."

Without thinking about it, my good hand slid over to cover the bad. Something I did on autopilot now anytime anyone even sort of glanced at my hands. As a way of saying, 'See, nothing special here.' The easiest of my flaws to spot, the hardest to lie about, and the one thing everyone was always asking about. Over the years, I'd gotten good at ignoring the questions rather than answering them.

"Simple, I had a motorcycle accident. My number got called, I went a bit nuts. Went out, bought a bike, drove it as fast as the thing would go on the most twisted road I could find. Which is easy around here. And flamed out big time. Saved myself from going to Nam but ended up with a lifetime of regrets." I nodded to myself at the sordid tale I'd made up on the spur of the moment all those years ago with Nancy. One that I'd embellished a great deal as time went on.

"And she believed that?" He twisted his lips, rather apparent he didn't buy it.

"Sure? Why not? She had no reason to doubt me. How long had she known me at that point? What? Long enough for me to guzzle a drink and not much more than that." I stared outside. A hint of light had begun to emerge from behind the dark clouds. The rain had eased up, people now roamed freely along the sidewalk. Going about their business once more. Normal day, nothing special going on for anyone other than me.

"Because your reaction seemed a bit extreme." He raised an eyebrow, "She makes one little comment and you break down in tears?"

The comment didn't do me in.

The jasmine did.

Not sure how to explain that. My mother's scent followed me everywhere I went. Or it turned out to be one of the most popular perfumes on the planet. When the scent hit me that night, I felt Nancy could be trusted. Because she had to be like my mother on some level. And therein lay my problem with oversharing. I feared being judged by yet another woman in my life.

"I do think at that moment my need to open up to someone had more to do with months of being alone. When one is trying to work through trauma, silence isn't golden. I'd been spinning events in a loop in my mind. Hoping to make something change, for something to click into place and put me together again. But that didn't happen, not for a very long time. And from what I can tell, not for a whole lot of other vets."

He gazed out the window for some time, digesting what I'd shared. "You ever visit one of those centers?" Still focused on the world beyond this room, not on me. "My father drank. He'd stand behind this bar, his drink under the counter. Pretend he had a glass of water. But it never was. Whiskey, rum, anything light so that it'd look like something it wasn't. But you could smell it on him. He'd claim he'd spilled something he'd served. Yet, I always knew it couldn't be true."

He swiveled his head to look at me again. "At one point, my mom told him she'd had enough. Told him to go get some help, talk to someone other than her. He went to a Vet Center for a while, or so he claimed. If you ask me, he just got better at hiding his drinking."

"That why you ended up in Florida?" I bit my lip.

Maybe I had things wrong about Lisa. She'd moved to the other side of the country and seldom called or visited us. I'd placed the blame for the rift in our family on my wife Nancy and her wagging tongue. However, children seem to always know what's going on in a house. Ryan's words were proof of that. I tried, Lord knows I did. But I'd been an angry, bitter man most of my adult life. Holding onto secrets made me feel I had no choice but to keep drinking for years. In the end, I do believe my efforts to change and be a better man had come too late. The damage to my child had already been done.

"At first, I told everyone I wanted to be somewhere warm for a change. Be near the ocean, play in the sand. Got a full ride to a school down there and never looked back. But I should've. It became too much for my mom to handle alone. She died of cancer before I graduated from college." He shook his head. The boy had more than his share of regrets it would seem.

"After her death, I didn't see any reason to come waltzing home and say 'hi' to my dad. Figured he'd be neck-deep in a bottle and wouldn't need me. We texted some over the next few years, nothing much really. Then last year he died. He needed help," Ryan waved around the room. "This all was beyond what he was capable of doing alone. I didn't have a clue as to how bad things were until I got here. Turns out the regulars were only hanging around for my dad. With him gone, nobody bothered to come in here anymore. I don't have any clue as to how to fix this mess, run a business, or what to do next. But I do think most of this is my fault. I shouldn't have abandoned them, or at the very least, I should've come back after my mother died." He sighed, long and deep. He took in a few deep breaths, his head lowered to his chest.

"Not sure you should put any of the blame on your shoulders young man. My best guess is your father saw things he couldn't deal with, same as I did. In my humble opinion, no soldier should have kids. We leave the worst kind of legacy behind. But that'd never work, now, would it? Then there'd never be a future since so many of us have served." I looked him up and down. "Your dad did more than ruin this bar, didn't he son?" I rushed on, not needing or wanting a reply. "Not sure if you go to church, or know any decent folks around here. But, it might help to talk to someone. Like I did once."

He nodded, but didn't give any sort of reply as he rubbed his knuckles together deep in thought.

Not wishing to shove Jesus down his throat, I pushed on. "But here you are now, the son of a drunk, running a bar into oblivion. Doing your part to prevent anyone else from becoming an alcoholic ever again." I slapped his arm, giving him a grin. "How's that for irony?"

"Alright then, what's your suggestion for this place?" He returned my smile with a goofy one of his own. "You've already convinced me I need to move on and do better with my life. So hit me with your best shot."

"Let me gnaw on that thought for a while, I'm not sure. Because it doesn't feel proper to hold AA meetings in a bar. But I might think of something, must be some other good use for this space." Waving an arm around, I gave the place a critical glance. Nothing came to me right off hand, well, other than the creeps from the dead animals staring at me.

"I'm not so sure any use for this ol' bar exists. You're more than likely right about me just needing to give up on this place." He also gazed around the space with a gleam in his eye.

I pulled something out of my pocket, laying it on the counter. "See this?"

He picked up the object, cradling it for a moment. "Is this the knife, the one you said you kept all those years?"

I accepted the knife back from him. "Yes. Some of the things we're given from our family we need to hold onto no matter what. Have you considered this building might be that thing for you?" I returned the knife back to its home in my jeans.

"Put a very big pin in those thoughts for now. It's not urgent, I've been holding onto this place for over a year now. Let's get back to you and your dilemma. You ready to face your daughter yet?" He patted the computer, tapping his fingers as he did.

How can I ever be ready to face Jenny? All of these years, all of the lies, all of the times my heart cried for her. Without knowing anything about her, I'd longed to see her face. And now I had. Well, a photo at least. "When my daughter Lisa was born, do you know what my first thought was?"

"No, what?" He tucked his hands into a fist, rapping on the counter as he did so.

"That she's the wrong child." I cringed. "Now, does that me the father of the year or what?"

He hesitated, scrunching up his eyes, moving his lips around. "No, I think it makes you a man who was grieving."

Huh, I'd never considered that possibility. "How did a young buck like you get so wise, Ryan?"

His face lit up as he turned to look at me fully, "Easy, I majored in psychology. Not like I ever worked in anything like that, after college I tended bar at a marina in Fort Lauderdale. Best job ever. Got to dress like a bum, make great money, and live on a boat."

Ah, and that was why he'd been chewing the fat with me all day. "Well, I do think your father and I were cut from the same cloth. Both vets, both drunks, both bad fathers. But unlike your father, God did grant me enough time to change my ways a mite."

"How so?" He raised an eyebrow.

"At some point, I listened to the sage advice of my daughter." An image of Lisa on the day she'd been born flooded my mind. I should've been happy, proud, excited about that moment. But I'm not that kind of man.

CHAPTER 12

Colorado – 1969 - Present Day

Nancy became my anchor, the one thing tying me to the earth, keeping me sane. For her, I stopped running—from my memories, from myself, from my past, from my pain.

Again, I'm not sure my feelings were love. More akin to finding a safe harbor to shelter me from the raging storm that my life had become. From those first few moments we'd met, I received nothing but acceptance from her. It wasn't for years that I learned she used this charm of hers as a weapon. A method to disarm people into divulging their deepest secrets. Which is how she always knew the juiciest gossip in town. And why she remained at the center of each and every rumor started. However, at first, she sucked me in, making me believe I would always be the one thing her world revolved around.

And I'd always get those little comments from her. She'd nag me for more details about my 'accident.' Oh, she was aware something more lay behind those few 'facts' I'd shared. But I stuck to my story, I wasn't anything more than a hick from the sticks who'd made a dumb move. I'd never been out of the country, never did anything interesting in my life, move on, stop asking questions.

On Christmas day, Nancy and I lingered at church after the service. Cuddling in the back row, enjoying a moment together in the glow of the candles from the service before we were supposed to snuff them out.

She pulled out a small box from her bright orange crochet bag, handing it to me with a shy smile. "I got you a gift."

We hadn't discussed exchanging presents; I didn't know what to do. "I'm sorry…"

She clasped my hand, leaning over to give me a quick kiss on my forehead. "No worries. Just a little something I picked up at a thrift store last week when I went to Denver on the beer run. Open it, you'll see that it's actually more for me."

I slid open the top, gold winking up at me. Looking closer at what lay inside, I spotted two simple bands. One small and one large, nestled on a bed of dark blue cloth. My body went cold, then hot. Without Nancy I didn't see how I could live, she'd propped me up in a way nothing else had.

But marriage?

"Why?" Not my finest hour, but not my worst either.

She turned my face toward hers, cupping my chin in her small hand. "Do you believe in the power of love to heal?"

I nodded yes, not sure if I truly believed it or not. However, this church we attended said something to that effect every time they met. I wanted it to be true.

"I want to give myself to you fully. But I can't if we aren't married. You've come a long way in the short time since we've met. You want your soul to finish healing, right? You want to become a true man of God, right?" Her bright eyes willing me to join her on a righteous quest to fulfill God's will for our lives.

What I needed was to be free from pain and heartbreak. At that moment, Nancy felt so safe and nurturing, I let myself believe her words were true. My first path had led me nowhere good. I'd abandoned my family, my pregnant girlfriend, what I thought I wanted in life. To end up in an unjust war. And land here a homeless bum.

But being with Nancy had been my fresh start. An opportunity to create the life I wanted, to build a world for the two of us. That first night in the bar, I'd felt like I had been drowning. She'd swooped in on a lifeboat, held out her hand, and pulled me in.

I couldn't jump out of the lifeboat now.

I'd sink and be lost forever.

"Nancy, will you marry me?" I pulled her close, stroking her hair.

"Yes, Bruce," she whispered in my ear.

We got married on New Year's Eve. A rather impromptu affair that neither of us planned, to be honest. Our little band of misfits we called a church had planned an event for the evening. Nancy viewed this to be the perfect time for us to become official. She didn't see any need to wait a second longer than necessary.

Our pastor got everything together in that week between Christmas and New Year's. Nothing had to change about the gathering, we were a mere afterthought. In the midst of the worship music, the pastor would pull us aside to a quiet corner at the time he believed to be best.

On New Year's Eve, we had a few hours before we planned to wander over to the church. Nancy and I sat snuggled on the couch before a roaring fire in the ski lodge. Despite the fact the hill would be having a 'midnight' run for skiers, almost no one had come. We had the place to ourselves as we sipped our hot chocolates and nibbled on the cookies she'd made.

"Are your parents coming tonight?" I'd been pondering on this question for a few days, she hadn't mentioned them at all. Wasn't sure if she wished to be respectful of me because mine were no longer living—well, as far as she knew, that is.

One of the lies that'd slipped out rather early in our relationship had been that both of my parents were dead. Don't even know why I'd gone there. Thus, I now couldn't go back and undo this, say, 'Oh, by the way, I misspoke, my mother isn't dead.' Which, yes, I did have more than a few tinges of guilt about the fact my mother would never know about my marriage. I think unconsciously I'd made my choice to never go back home, too much had happened. My heart kept telling me the best move to make would be to keep going forward and never look back. To try to avoid the same fate as Lot's wife from the Bible. Because to me, as bad as things were, going home could only serve to compound my issues.

But that didn't stop those ghosts from haunting me.

"To what? The potluck?" She giggled, pushing herself deeper into my arms. "Honest, no. My mother's too sick to travel. And for what? Our little part of this will take, what? Five minutes?"

I stroked her dark hair, picking my next words with care. In the end, I choose to ignore how flippant she'd been about our impending vows. "Aren't you from here?"

"Oh, goodness no!" She struggled to sit up straighter, looking right at me. "I thought you knew. I'm from back east."

No, she'd never mentioned that, not once. But then again, this explained why she hadn't questioned my lie about being from around here. This being such a small area, I'd figure that one would catch up to me at some point or another.

"So how'd you end up here?" Wrapping my arms around her once again, I drew her back in.

"By accident." She sighed, "Do you really want to hear the story? It's not very interesting."

"Sure I do, my love." I kissed the top of her head.

"Okay, fine, whatever. Last summer, I joined a bunch of war protesters and ended up in San Francisco. But that first time we stood outside the fence shouting at the soldiers getting off the plane…" Her voice grew faint, her body gave a shiver against mine. "I stood so close I could see the pain in their eyes at our words. We weren't being fair. We were shouting and being angry at the wrong people. The government's to blame for this stupid war, not the poor guys who get their number called."

And I knew exactly what she was talking about. Had her voice been one of those I'd heard when I'd stepped off the plane? Had I seen her in the crowd as I tried so hard to ignore those hateful words? I tipped her face up to look into her watery eyes, and she reached up to wipe a drop from mine. This bond we shared, I could never reveal. Or had the time come for me to come clean? Tell her the truth and beg for her forgiveness? In a few hours, we'd be man and wife, one person, not two. How could I not be honest?

"Sorry, you're thinking of your buddy who died over there. I shouldn't have said anything." She shifted her weight and started to rise. I clasped her hand, yanking on it so she'd have to stay put.

"It's fine, finish what you were going to tell me." I gave her a grim hint of a smile, believing she'd just given me permission to not say more. To not share what lay on my heart and mind.

She perched on the edge of the cushion. "Well, I went back to the hostel and started to throw my things in my bag. On the floor, I spotted a newspaper, don't know why for sure, but I picked it up. The Denver Post. I'll never forget that. Someone had left it open to the classifieds, and had circled a notice for help at a bar. I called the number, collect no less. The person who answered told me I had the job if I showed up ready to work in two days. And that's how I ended up here, in this magical spot, hidden from the world. The bar hadn't been in Denver at all."

"What did your parents think about that?" I rubbed her straight back, trying to ease her tension. Something didn't add up, but I couldn't put my finger on it.

"They think I'm one of those dope-smoking hippies who lives in a commune or a van. Oh, and who sleeps with every man I meet. But I'm not." She put a soft hand on my face, leaning in to give me a kiss. "And I never will be. I'm yours and yours alone."

We chatted for a while longer before she told me she had to go finish getting ready for the evening.

Later at church, I stood near the entrance waiting for her. Still wearing my best bell-bottomed jeans, the only pair without holes. A white T-shirt under my favorite red flannel shirt. My feet shod with a new pair of cowboy boots. This was as fancy as I got.

Nancy rushed in buried under layers of wool coat, hat, gloves, and mittens. It'd been snowing all day, almost everyone had arrived bundled up. The food for the potluck had been covered in blankets to try to keep it warm.

I watched as Nancy peeled off her outer layers, revealing a white peasant top and a quilted skirt. She twirled in a circle around me as she drew near. "You like my outfit? I made the skirt myself from scraps, it's my something old, something new, and my something blue. The blouse is borrowed. I'm all set!"

"You look amazing." I wrapped an arm around her waist, kissing her cheek.

The music started—loud, praise Jesus at the top of your lungs songs. Everyone danced, sang, a great time to be had by one and all. No formal dinner setting or tables to eat at, people snacked when they got hungry. This evening was more about being together to celebrate another year we'd been given. And to ask for the Lord's favor in the year that was to come. Then came the tap on my shoulder, a nod from the pastor. Our moment had come.

Saying our vows at the stroke of midnight, we rang in the new with our lives forever joined together.

Sure, we'd been dating for all of a few months, and nothing more than a few chaste kisses had happened yet. Because I for darn sure wasn't going to make the same mistake twice. Either I'd do right by Nancy or I'd leave her in the dust. No more rendezvous in seedy motel rooms for me. She'd told me I'd be her first, I told her the same. Seemed easier to pile on another lie than to go telling her about what I'd left behind in Texas.

And the words of that chaplain from Fort Sam rang in my head, 'You can't undo the past, you can't right a wrong. But you can move forward and never make the same mistake twice.' It became my mantra as I moved into my new life with Nancy.

I'd convinced myself I could, and would, do better with this second chance I'd been given. Not only had I been given the gift of a wife, but the gift of my life when I could've just as easily met the same fate as that corpsman.

By then, I'd managed to wrangle a job with the state. Nothing much, working in the state parks at one of their campgrounds. It'd keep me outside, keep me busy, and keep my mind occupied. Nancy claimed she'd be happy enough giving up her job at the bar to head out with me to my assigned spot. Working there had been a means to an end for her.

Do believe she'd been scouting for a man for a while, and for reasons that eluded me, I'd been her choice. And now, she wanted to be my assistant with my many chores at the park. Cleaning the restrooms. Prepping sites for the next campers. Chopping wood to sell. Picking up trash. Or to simply be the one who'd chat with the many families who'd come to enjoy nature.

We didn't have a honeymoon; we went from the party at the church to my campsite. Didn't matter to us dawn would be breaking soon. Nestling in under the covers, snug as two little bugs could be. Or at least, as cozy as anyone can make a topper on the back of a truck. I'd strung a few paper streamers before I'd headed out that afternoon, most of which had fallen down either coming or going. But the 'welcome home' sign remained over the door, and she smiled as she entered.

She soon learned the joys of always having your home with you. On our second day of marriage, she didn't realize she had to tuck her dishes away. The resulting destruction left her weeping for hours, not a plate or glass left unscathed.

We left the campsite that morning, driving the truck, of course. When we returned to our assigned spot that night, we opened the topper door. To discover utter chaos because everything not put in its place had gone flying each time I turned a corner. Shards of china and glass were everywhere. I found a fork stuck in a wall. I cleaned the mess for her, letting her relax in the front cab as I did. But her wails came to me through the thin metal wall. For whatever reason she'd become inconsolable over something this trivial.

Thus, it didn't take long before I traded my truck camper for a small Airstream. Again, nothing fancy but large enough for two. Tiny 'bedroom' in the back with a coarse curtain to separate the space from the remainder of the trailer. A minuscule bathroom with a toilet and a shower had been placed in the middle. And a kitchen/living room in the front by the lone door. Fridge, sink, stovetop, table with two bench seats.

The important thing here, it disconnected from the truck.

We built a little world for the two of us over the course of the remaining winter. Fixing up that trailer and making it a true home for us, which was much easier to do when we didn't have to move it after placing it on site. Nancy found a few multi-colored throw pillows at the local thrift store. An old faded pink bedspread she turned into curtains. A few knick-knacks she placed in strategic spots. Someone surprised us with a photo of the instant we'd kissed at midnight. They'd thought we'd looked so cute and didn't know until later the significance of the moment.

I found an old steel barrel I turned into a fire pit. Added to that a small sink I found at the dump and we had an outdoor kitchen in no time. We'd be set for summer when the spring thaw finally broke. Living in a campground would be our paradise, a tiny world for us as we found our way as newlyweds.

She turned out to be a former faithful Protestant. I never once mentioned my Catholic upbringing. However, she'd swung toward the evangelical side of things. To a church where emotion ruled and traditions were thrown out the window.

There we'd be, each Sunday at nine A.M. like clockwork for service. We'd sit in the last row of chairs in the back, more comfortable for me to be near the door. Our Bible open on our laps, having a Jesus revolution moment with everyone else in the room.

Rock and roll worship rang out, loud and strong, from a mashed-together band with guitars and drums. I found it rather unsettling, to say the least.

Open confessions as one and all laid everything they'd ever done on the altar, giving everything to God. Words which should've been spoken in private to a priest were shared for all to hear, I tried to block them out.

I had enough problems of my own to deal with, thank you very much.

A fiery message which didn't always come from the pastor; if one of us felt so led to speak, that wasn't a problem at all. Lots and lots of tears flowed as these mostly new believers felt the power of the Holy Spirit move with a mighty rushing wind. Expecting great things because God was good, God was love, and God would provide.

But I knew better.

I knew that God wasn't all sunshine and rainbows. I'd deserted the mother of my child. I'd seen innocent children wounded. I'd seen a man die before my eyes. Thus, how much love could God possibly have for the world?

Not much as far as I could tell.

Many in the group were former war protestors from California or elsewhere around the country. They'd come to realize hate couldn't be an answer to the war. Many were former drug addicts who'd been healed and delivered. Or refugees from the hippie communes now looking for a better path than free love. Wherever we'd come from, we were all people seeking solace in a world that no longer made sense to any of us.

But finding peace isn't that easy, or at least, not for me.

Given the group of people Nancy had come west with, it made sense she'd gravitated towards this type of expression of faith. She'd been pushing against her upbringing to join the protesters in the first place. When that didn't turn out to be what she needed, she had to find another outlet. For her, she understood where the others had been, because she'd been there as well.

Me, no, not so much. I hadn't found my faith in a foxhole, I'd lost it. To be honest, I'd begun to let go of the bonds of family and faith while I was in college. All because I'd tried to fit in with others who didn't have any answers. I'd thought following the confused masses would turn out better than continuing along the straight and narrow. Why, I didn't have any clue. Now, I went to church to please my wife. Not because a tug in my soul led me to do so.

We fit in this group as well as could be expected. After all, we looked the part to the outside world. Many an evening they'd join us in the woods, singing praise songs around a campfire. Didn't matter if the snow was falling or not. They were needing something more from life. A need to change the world into a place that would be safe, filled with peace and love.

We all looked, acted, and sounded like a bunch of hippies. Most of us men had long hair and beards. We wore worn-out jeans and T-shirts. Half of us didn't wear shoes unless the snow was falling. The women often put flowers in their hair to match their long skirts. But what set those in our church apart from so many others of our generation was faith.

They had a belief in something greater than themselves. A belief that God still cared for His children. That He still wanted to draw near to them. And most of all, that He still wanted to bring joy to this world that had been ravaged by war.

As for me, I went along with the wave of Nancy's whims. From her bout of decorating to her faith. Because I also needed something to hold onto. Something different, a major change in my life. I needed something to give me a sense of peace.

But the nightmares didn't end. They may have faded a bit as I welcomed Nancy into my life. But I woke more nights than I cared to admit in a full-blown panic. And in the tiny space I shared with my new bride, hiding my drinking wasn't possible.

By March, Nancy announced we'd become three. My gut instinct had been the same as the first time, as on the day Donna told me the same words, 'I'm pregnant.'

Run, run as fast and far as possible, and never look back. No longer the scared kid I'd been a year ago, I'd now become a damaged man whose demons might very well destroy his wife and child. So much had changed in one short year. And yet, nothing much had. Time had looped, come back on repeat, forcing me to make a different choice this time.

So I did. Although not willingly at first.

On that Sunday morning at breakfast, Nancy had fixed me a breakfast full of 'baby' food. Baby potatoes, eggs, mini muffins.

She placed the plate in front of me, grabbed my hand, and rubbed her stomach with it. "You ready for our next chapter?"

I didn't say anything, I didn't look up at her, my mind racing hoping beyond hope she didn't mean what I thought she meant.

"Silly, I'm pregnant." She patted my hand which she continued to clutch against her abdomen.

I almost blurted out, 'How?' but managed to stop myself just in time. Instead, I pulled her into my lap, kissing her with all I had in me. Which turned out to be a mistake.

"You're drunk." She pushed away from me for a second, giving me a good, hard stare.

"No, I had a nip of cough syrup. The cold air this morning made my throat hurt." I returned her glare with one of my own. And yanked her back in to resume my smooching. She didn't resist, so I figured she'd bought my latest lie.

After more than a few minutes of making out, we managed to separate ourselves. We scarfed down our breakfast and headed out to church. Upon our arrival, we settled into our chairs as normal, nothing out of the ordinary as far as I was concerned.

For my wife, oh, that morning was another story. As the worship band got into full swing, several others got into full 'Holy Ghost' mode. They were laid out on the floor howling for all they were worth, writhing as was often the case. Nancy tugged on my arm. I lowered my raised hand, giving her a glance.

She nodded to me, leaning over to whisper, "It's your turn to be healed." And she started to shove me out into the aisle.

Motioning to a few others around us, before long I became surrounded by other worshipers. And to my horror, they seemed to know an awful lot about my personal life.

"Lord, heal our brother from the evils of drink!"

"Lord, heal his mind from the demons that torment him each night as he dreams!"

"Lord, heal his heart from the lies he holds close!"

It went on forever, some began to speak in tongues, others chanting scriptures over me. For reasons I didn't understand, I began to sway as these good people laid their hands upon me. My eyes filled with tears.

Hands gently guided me down to the floor, leaving me sitting with my arms curled around my knees. I felt the pressure of a firm hand on mine, as the man's other hand gripped my shoulder hard. He began to whisper in my ear, so soft at first I didn't understand.

"Bruce, you were given free will." His words hit me, startling me with their forcefulness. "Same as all men. We know that evil comes. The question is why?" I now knew the voice, our pastor. His hand gripped mine tighter, "Son, if nothing bad ever happened then we wouldn't have to make a choice. Because it does, we have the free will to choose. God or evil? What are you going to pick today?"

This summed up what I'd been wrestling with for months. The question of 'why?' Why had I experienced so much, done so many things wrong, hurt this much, caused so much harm to others?

Was this my answer? On one level this appeared to be so basic, even a child should've been aware of it. Yet, on another, it felt profound, as if God Himself had just spoken to me. The answer lay in what we as men decide to do with our lives. My decisions had led me here, to this place. This had nothing to do with God and everything to do with me.

My mind filled with visions of what life could be like without my nightmares. Without needing the crutch of alcohol to sleep. And for a moment, I believed in the power of God to fix my deepest wounds and scars. Not those on my hand but the ones in my heart, my mind, my soul.

I wanted more than life itself to make a different choice this time.

"God." I said the words; I wanted and needed them to be true.

And over the course of the next few months, I became a pillar of the community, a leader in the church. But most important, the husband and soon-to-be father the world expected of me.

The elderly widow needs her roof fixed? No problem, I'd rustle up a couple of guys on my day off and buy the supplies with my hard-earned money. Have her house looking like new in no time.

The kids need a camp counselor? I got that as well, I'm already in the campground. Practically don't even have to leave my backyard to help with that.

The church building needs to be cleaned after service? I'm your man. In my mind, idle thoughts were the devil's playground. Hence, my previous issues had been all a matter of having too much time on my hands. I'd never make that mistake again.

However, the weight of all these new burdens I'd piled on proved to be too much for me to carry. I'd been incorrect, my invisible wounds couldn't be buried, ignored, forgotten, as I did busy work. No, they had to be dealt with, worked through, faced head-on. And my world came crashing down because I didn't understand any other way to cope with what lay hidden than to find solace at the bottom of a bottle.

The more Nancy's pregnancy progressed, the sicker she became. Most days, we'd be lucky if she got out of bed for an hour or two. Even with the help from the other women in our church, and with the prayers from everyone, I didn't see how we'd make it through this crisis.

And my demons returned in a crashing wave. Resulting in me hitting the booze yet again somewhere in her seventh month.

The more time that passed the bigger my façade became. All to hide my lies, which were getting layered on like so much manure on a pile in an old barn. That other child of mine Donna had the year before. My nightmares from Nam which now came more often than ever.

The healing session at the church hadn't been anything more than a band-aid. My wounds remained raw, open, bleeding.

My drinking numbed me and helped me to manage everything. What other choice did I have than to present a false front to everyone? To pretend I was someone I wasn't? None. Absolutely none from what I'd learned about myself at that point. I'd let things go too long to allow even one little bit of the truth to come out now.

Early in October, Nancy woke me from a dead sleep. I'd had a bit too much to drink after dinner, and ended up passing out on the bench at the kitchen table watching Bonanza. Not a first for me, nor would it be the last time.

In my groggy state, her words, "It's time," didn't quite register at first.

"We just finished dinner, I'm not hungry." I swatted at the hand she tugged on my leg with.

"No, silly goose. The baby's coming. I made coffee." She plopped a lukewarm mug on the table in front of me. "Hurry, before I double over again."

After a ginger gulp or two of the wicked-strong stuff, I unpeeled my eyes. Staring at her as she leaned on the only bit of counter space in our trailer, heaving and panting in a weird rhythm. Labor, she's having labor pains. And here I sat half in the bag. Finishing the coffee, I grabbed her coat—mine I didn't bother with. But she needed one, she still wore her flimsy light blue nightie. Not the good dark maroon flannel one she'd worn most of the winter. No, that had gotten way too small for her as her belly had expanded.

I stood in our small space, wearing my clothes from the day before, work boots and all. Without any argument from her, I got her into the truck and headed out. At the local hospital, the nurses took one look at her, popped her into a wheelchair, and whisked her off. Once I had the truck parked, I'd been escorted to the 'fathers' room.'

I paced that waiting area, in worried tension for my second child to be born. Well, I'd alternated between being perched on the blue and white checkered couch and wearing out the faded green-speckled linoleum for hours. My whole body a taut spring, waiting for something to happen which would release the pressure I was under.

But the time on the clock spun and still no one came to speak a word to ease my suffering. The faint green of the walls had calmed me at first, when the situation didn't seem so dire. Daylight had entered the room at some point, then vanished. At this moment, the sole light remaining came from the dim glow emitting from the single almost burnt-out bulb in the overhead light. The result left the color of the walls to appear rather ghoulish and off.

One of the women, a nurse, asked if I had someone I wished to call at one point. I didn't know who she'd been, she hadn't been dressed in white. And I didn't pay much attention; to be honest, I wouldn't even have been able to recall what her hair color might have been. I'd shook my head 'no' at her question, but I now regretted that choice.

Someone, anyone from our church should've been here. This I

couldn't deal with on my own. Because most of the time I'd spent in this tiny space I hadn't been thinking of my wife. Nor had my thought been on our baby she was about to give birth to. No, my thoughts kept drifting back to Donna.

I took a few sips of whiskey from my flask. Shaking it a bit, I realized I didn't have much left. The buzz the stuff gave me hadn't been enough to keep the visions of Donna out of my head.

I'd tried to pray, but no words would form. I'd tried to focus on the life I'd built with Nancy. But I kept picturing Donna's face the day she told me she was pregnant. I'd robbed her of the child she'd wanted so much.

Had anyone been available for Donna other than some nun or nurse? Had she been able to look at the child at least once before handing him or her over to strangers? Where had our child ended up? How had he or she spent their first birthday? Were his or her new parents kind? Nice? Nurturing? Was he or she an only child? My heart ached knowing I didn't have any connection to that child. That I'd soon be holding a baby in my arms but in many respects, it'd be the wrong one.

"Son?" An older gentleman stood in the doorway leading into the depths of the hospital. Dressed in green scrubs and a white coat, his posture straight and tall. "I'm Dr. Hamilton."

I nodded as I took a hesitant step his way, unable to speak. Pushing my flask deep into the pocket of my jeans, I dug out a mint. Popping it in my mouth, I plastered on the best smile I could.

"Mom and baby are doing fine. Both are a bit tired after such a long delivery but I can take you to meet your daughter if you want." He clapped me on the back hard, shaking my hand till I was sure it'd fall off.

"Thank you." My voice shaky, weak. A wave of relief washed over me, thankful that Nancy would be okay. But much more grateful I'd no longer be trapped alone in this tiny room with my depressing thoughts.

I'd wished for a son in the long months I'd watched our child grow inside Nancy, a boy I would raise to be a better man than me. But, in the end, I figured this daughter would be better. She wouldn't want to copy anything I'd do. She'd take after her mother instead.

We pushed through the swinging doors together; a whole sterile world lay beyond. I followed the doctor down the long, white hallway, our footsteps echoing in the silence. These sounds filled the emptiness that is a large building in the wee hours of the morning.

Nancy had gone into labor almost twenty-four hours previously, and I'd been kept in the dark for most of that time. All I'd been told had been something about 'complications.' Did I agree to any and all 'lifesaving measures?' In addition, someone would explain later. However, later never seemed to come.

Turning a corner, a wall made of glass stood before us. Dr. Hamilton pulled me close, pointing to one of the tiny bundles. This one had been wrapped up tight in a pink blanket. "That's your little precious gift." He slapped my back again. "You and the misses have any ideas for names yet?"

I shook my head 'No,' unsure what to say. I started to brush the tears away, but no point in that. They were coming too fast. As I leaned my head on the glass, his hand squeezed my shoulder, the pressure strong and sure. This, this is what I'd given up. I'd created a gift of life with Donna. One which I'd tossed aside so callously, so cruelly. How do I find a way to ever make up for that mistake? I guess by being the best father ever for this new little creature who lay so innocently in the basket before me.

But I'm a flawed man. My child would've been better off with someone else.

I tried to focus on what little of my daughter I could see. Her wee little nose, her small eyes shut tight against the bright lights of the room, her pale lips puckered in a pout. A woman in a starched white uniform walked over to the edge of the bassinet. With great care, as if the sleeping child were made of porcelain, she picked up the bundle.

Gliding to the window, she held my daughter as close to the glass as possible. She pulled a fragile hand out from under the covers, showing me these five minuscule fingers. So perfect, something too wonderful to have any connection with me. The woman turned, with the same gentleness as before, and returned my child to her bed.

"We need to let her be for a bit longer. Let's go to a quiet place to talk for a moment. Fine by you, son?" He tugged on my arm, he wasn't going to take no for an answer. My hand slid down the glass to my side as I straightened my posture to the best of my ability.

We strolled down another corridor, I spotted a trash can tucked in a corner. Pulling my flask from my pocket, I slipped it into the waiting receptacle. This had to be the first step in becoming a good father. Not drinking, not hiding booze in every little corner I found.

We rounded another corner and ended up in a room that had to be the chapel. He took slow, measured steps to the altar. Kneeling, he made the sign of the cross before bending his head a moment.

Standing lost for a second, I wasn't sure what I should do. I was no longer Catholic. And I didn't want any questions to arise later if I repeated what the doctor had just done. Before I decided what to do, he rose and took a seat in the front pew. Patting the rich blue velvet of the bench, he smiled up at me. I sat as well, my hands crossed in my lap.

He placed a hand on my shoulder, soft, light touch. I understood what information he had to impart wasn't going to be good. "Son," he coughed, "There's no good way to say this. Your wife went into distress during the delivery, and we had to rush her into surgery." I guess my face betrayed my raging emotions, because he rushed on. "No, don't worry. Like I said before, she's going to be fine. But the thing is, she won't be able to have more children."

All of my pent-up breath came out in a whoosh. This wasn't bad news at all. This might be the best news ever, if I were to be honest. Not like I'd have ever admitted that to anyone. "What happens now?"

"She's going to need a lot of time to heal. You'll need to do most of the caring for the baby at first. Are you up for that?" His grip tightened, his kind face softened.

Nodding, my mind raced. We didn't have much of a plan for the baby, and now I'd be the one to have to figure everything out? The universe had to be playing some kind of joke on me, making me pay double for what I'd done. "Yes sir."

"Good to hear. Let's remain here for a while, pray together, if you don't mind. Then, I'll take you up to see your wife. Yes?" He continued to squeeze his hand, giving my upper arm quite the workout.

Again, my only response had been to nod. We continued to sit in the quiet chapel for what seemed like an eternity, his lips moving in silent prayer. When he'd finished, he rose, motioning me to follow.

Wandering into the halls once again, I stayed a step behind. The final corridor we entered had been dimmed, most of the overhead lights now off. A large desk appeared before us and doorways mushroomed around it. Dr. Hamilton waved to a nurse behind the counter as we walked by, not slowing in the least. He pushed open a door, allowing me to enter, but he turned to leave.

"Doctor?" I reached for the door but stopped when I saw the look of sadness on his face.

"It's up to you now son. The nurses will help all they can." The door closed with a soft thump as he let go of the handle.

The low light of the room made it difficult to see Nancy at first. I approached the bed with more than a bit of caution. The gynecologist in Nam had said something about bad deliveries being similar to the trauma from war. I almost didn't want to look. Her skin no longer had her usual warm glow; now as she lay still as a stone, she blended in with the white sheets. Plopping into the chair beside the bed, I swept her hand into mine. Making a vow to myself to do whatever it took to bring her back to health again.

A week later, I found myself bringing my girls home. Mother and daughter both were doing as well as could be expected given the situation. I'd cleaned the trailer from top to bottom, inside and out. The women from the church had agreed to bring meals several times a day for a few weeks. All in an effort to help us get into the swing of being a family. My job didn't seem to mind that I now did my rounds in the park with a baby strapped to my back. Life settled into an odd sort of routine, and Nancy came back to life, with each slow and painful step.

Turns out, raising a child in a tiny travel trailer isn't the best idea. It also seems that quitting drinking wasn't something I was capable of doing even for the sake of my daughter. As I moved up the ranks at my job, we were able to adjust our living situation.

We bought a house. Which was much more compatible with the needs and wants of a growing little girl. Yet, even her bright, sunny smile couldn't chase away my nightmares. By her second birthday, I'd started needing a drink or four on most nights.

In fact, in many ways, I do think Lisa made things worse for me. Not that I blame her for my inability to deal with life in general. However, I'd look at her and wonder about my missing child. Which was wrong in so many ways. Did the two of them have anything in common? Would they meet accidentally someday? All of the milestones that Lisa hit, I'd have a moment I'd wonder about that other child as well.

And I became an angry, bitter man who drank in secret to cope with everything.

Which didn't escape Nancy's watchful eye. And these times would pop up when she'd make a comment, ask me to drink less, or suggest I seek counseling from our pastor. Nothing big, little digs or jabs thrown at me as off remarks. Until my drinking started to affect my job.

"Dear, we need to talk." Nancy greeted me at the door of the house, blocking me from entering.

I'd come home late, again, because I'd stopped at the bar, again. After having spent the day on the lake fishing and drinking, again. I didn't wish to discuss anything, what I wanted to do was go to my study and flop onto the couch and watch the late show. "Not tonight, okay, hun? Tomorrow, yeah?"

She plopped her ever-widening backside onto the top step, "No, now. Dan called, wanted to know how you're feeling since you've been sick all week."

Uh, oh. I'd decided to use up my time off by having some time to myself. Didn't see the harm, until now. Should've known I'd get caught since my boss was as much of a gossip as my wife. "About that..."

"Look, you've got a wife and a six-year-old daughter to support. You can't do that if you're drunk. I've been patient, I've prayed, I've called on everyone else to pray. But you've got to do the work." She put her hands between her knees, making the skirt of her red dress dip down to the ground.

I sank beside her, unsure how to respond. "Why are you here?" I looked over at her, asking almost the same question of her that Susan had asked of me so long ago.

"To get you to stop drinking, I already said that." She huffed.

I reached out to stroke her leg, "No, I meant in this marriage. Take Lisa, go somewhere, anywhere, where you don't have me as a stone around your neck."

She stared out into the night, her eyes focused on something across the street. Her chin tilted up, her lips pursed as if she was about to speak.

After a long pause, she switched her gaze towards me. "I'd have to say because God sent me to save you. It's my job to make sure you get the miracle you need. I guess you don't realize that from the day we met, it's been you and me against the world. Sure, my parents are still alive, but they want nothing to do with me. You are the one I'm supposed to comfort, nurture, love. To leave you would be to deny you the healing that God wishes to bestow upon you. You're the lost penny I had to find, pick up from the ground, and keep forever."

Something in this logic of hers sounded twisted and off, but my inebriated brain couldn't figure out what. However, since my reasons for being married weren't the greatest either I had no right to judge.

Deep inside, a part of me was aware that if I hadn't found her, I'd have killed myself. More than likely in a slow and painful accidental way out in the wilderness alone. And to leave her now would prove to the world I'd never been a man because I'd have abandoned two children if I did. No, I'd made my bed and now lay stuck in it whether I liked it or not.

And I got sober again. For a few years.

Not sure when exactly, but I swung back into old habits. The nightmares became too painful to face, the memories came without warning. Needing my crutch, I dove back into the nearest bottle. Hard. But by then, I figured I'd learned enough to keep the evidence hidden.

As Nancy and I aged and matured, the world around us did as well. Our church and its members mellowed. Almost all of us ended up having children, more than a few, to be honest. The services became less intense, less loud.

By the mid-eighties, emotions were less the focus. Intensive study of the Bible was done instead. I continued to play my part in life, accepting the hand I'd allowed myself to be dealt. I worked hard, continued to be a leader in the community and church as well. My secrets were mine and mine alone. Or so I fervently hoped they were.

"Dad, I don't want you to be a camp counselor this year." Lisa entered my home office one afternoon, on a perfect early spring day. She looked so grown up now that she'd started taking high school classes at the local Christian academy.

She stood before me in her dark navy-blue uniform, which consisted of a skirt and blazer, a white button-down shirt underneath.

Her dark brown hair she'd pulled back with a red ribbon. We'd homeschooled her until this year, at Nancy's insistence. Most of the kids at our church had been taught in the same manner. Public schools couldn't be trusted because prayer wasn't allowed.

"Why, honey?" I looked up at her from the report I'd been filling out, nothing important. Another stupid idiot at the campground had lit a small brush fire. All because he didn't use the fire ring in his assigned camping spot. Over the years, I'd seen hundreds of these types of incidents, I was sure.

"Uhm, okay. How do I put this and still be respectful?" Her slim frame bounced from one foot to the other. Her red Keds her sole act of rebellion against the standard uniform. "We all know what's in your canteen, Dad. And we don't think it's appropriate."

Her words hit me like a slap. I gripped the edge of my desk, pulling myself closer to it. Yup, kids always know. They hear the fights parents have, even when those sharp words are whispered not shouted. And they know something isn't right when you won't share your water on a hike.

"Understood." Should I plead my case, whine about how I'll try to do better? Yet, how many times in the past had I tossed out the bottle? Like the day I'd learned of her imminent arrival, or the day of her birth, or the dozens of other times over the years? Only to end up crawling back into the nearest bottle the next time I hit a bump in the road. Because those nightmares never left. The blood and gore always flashed before my eyes.

"Dad, who were you before you met Mom?" Her innocent eyes gazed right into mine, diving deep into my soul. Willing me to come clean, to no longer hide my true self.

However, if I couldn't bring myself to tell Nancy the whole story, I for darn sure couldn't tell some teenager. "I mean, you never have answered my questions about what my grandparents might have been like. You don't have a single photo or anything."

She knew everything, just like her mother had always known. That what I said about myself was nothing but a pack of lies. "Someone you wouldn't have wanted to know," I whispered, more an answer to my internal struggle than to the child standing before me.

As I rose, I made a decision, one I should've made years before. To sober up, once and for all. Not by having people 'pray' for me. Not by removing the alcohol from my life. But by going to a professional and getting the help I should've sought from the very beginning. God and I might've become friends over the years, but this step had to be up to me.

I started going to a counselor a few towns over, and ended up in AA. Between the two, I figured out a way to clean up my act, almost twenty years too late. The interesting thing I discovered in doing this was that my faith blossomed. I came to see God in a whole new light. As a loving Father, willing to accept me, flaws and all.

Yet, even with these new revelations into my circumstances, I never did reveal everything. I didn't mention Nam, I didn't mention Donna. Some things no one needed to know. Didn't matter how many times they reminded me at the AA meeting that everything shared was in confidence. My secrets had to remain locked in the vault I'd kept them in for so long.

CHAPTER 13

Colorado – Present Day

"Wait, what?" Ryan looked over at me, his eyes wide, his mouth open. "You don't drink? But I've been giving you beer after beer…"

"Until today, I haven't touched a drop since nineteen eighty-four. But given what I'm facing today, it seemed like the perfect day to fall off the wagon. Throw away every damn chip I've earned over the years." I reached over to grab my mug. I raised my tankard high, giving him a pretend toast. Then gulped the remaining few drops.

"Your daughter finding you after all these years doesn't seem like enough. Not to give up something like forty years of sobriety to me." He grabbed the mug out of my hand, throwing it at the back wall.

Not flinching in the least at the shattering of the glass, I let out a laugh. "Ah, but you're forgetting the bit about my tour in Nam. And the fact that Nancy and Lisa don't know anything about my previous life. Yup, a whole lot of memories have been stuffed deep inside me for a whole lot of years. So, my dear young man, waltz around that bar and pour me another." I started to reach out for his half-filled mug.

"Not on your damn life am I giving you even one drop more. I'm cutting you off." He snatched his glass, sending it along the same trajectory as mine. Resulting in almost the same fate. Because his hadn't been empty, the liquid splashed over half the room. Including us.

"Fine, have it your way." I continued to chuckle as I shook my hands to get the beer off. Then stopped short.

Something began to gnaw at the back of my brain about then— who'd been the match for the DNA test? A dim light from the far reaches of my brain grew brighter as the realization came into focus.

No one from back in the day had any idea where I had landed. Thus, this mystery link couldn't be some random second or third cousin, once or twice removed. My email, unlike almost everyone else on the planet, had nothing to do with my name. Nor did it include my birth year or graduation year, or nickname.

Nor anything else someone might be able to figure out by some lucky guess. Only one explanation remained. Only one common link had been formed between me and this newly found daughter.

"Ryan, can ya pull up that email again?" Knowing the answer already, yet not wanting to admit it at all.

He stretched over to grab the abandoned computer, tapping a few things to get it to respond. "You ready to send that reply now? And to stop being a stupid, stubborn ass sitting here drinking all day?"

Biting the edge of my knuckle, I kept my mouth shut, refusing to utter a word. But all that beer swirled inside me, rising to the top and threatening to spew out. My secret already had found its way into the cold light of day and the truth now lay in the hands of someone. One person held the key to all of this. Why this hadn't clicked in my brain earlier, I didn't have a clue.

Glancing at the email again, the answer lay nestled deep in those black and white lines, right at the bottom. My daughter, no, my *daughters* had connected. They'd found each other. And together decided what the best move would be upon learning who they were to each other.

Lisa had given Jenny my email address thinking it'd be less stressful for me to hear the news in that form. My heart broke as I came to the realization of what Lisa must now think of me. Of what I did in the past. Of what other secrets she might think I'm still keeping.

In the end, all of this had been my fault. Because I gave up one child, I hid my life from another. Thus, in the end, Lisa had too many unanswered questions. How could I fault her for trying to find out who she was by doing a DNA test?

She'd wanted to find grandparents, aunts, uncles, cousins, a connection to her past. Instead, she found a half-sister. And in the process discovered her father had been nothing but a pretty façade hiding a whopper of a mess.

Another lightning bolt hit me, every ounce of me on fire. If my child knew, had she told her mother, my wife? Odds were no. A whole lot of reasons lay behind Lisa's decision to live on the other side of the country, her mother being one of them. And as I'd now come to believe, so was I. Thank goodness for small favors that Nancy and Lisa weren't close.

"Look, you see this, Ryan? Jenny, the child I gave up, and Lisa, the daughter I raised, have been chatting online. There's no going back now. I have to see this through. Can I use your computer to send an email to my wife to tell her I'm going on a bit of a trip?" A wave of excitement washed over me; I tingled in anticipation of meeting Jenny. Of seeing her in person, not as some image on a computer screen.

A flash of my childhood home flooded my brain, my mother standing on the porch, ringing the bell for dinner. My dozens of cousins and I would come running, my mother being the best cook for miles. She'd always fix a feast, even if the food was the simple fare from the farm. Roast chicken, fresh potatoes, peas and carrots from the field, fresh wheat bread she'd baked that morning.

Family gathered round the big table out in the backyard. Didn't matter if that included the boys who might be helping in the fields that week. And I'd given that up to go to college, to hang out with the guys doing weed. And then I'd gone even further.

Where this began had to be my next step. The time had come to bring everything full circle.

"Uhm, to where?" He gave me a questioning stare, eyebrows raised.

"Texas." My voice firm, steady, sure. This felt right. For the first time in a long time, I had a plan to fix something, not break it.

"Whoa." He gave a bit of grimace, "Dude, your wife deserves more than an email, I'm sure. Look, I get that you're still in overload mode, but I can't be the only one who knows the whole story. She deserves the truth."

"Right now I can't do anything for my wife. She'll have to wait, or ask Lisa questions." I rapped on the wooden top, sure my idea would put me on the right path. For once in my life, I felt in my core I knew what I should do.

"Understood." He gave me a long look, tapping his fingers on his chin. "But I still think you should call her. Now I'm going to go in the back for a minute to give you some privacy to think about what you need to say." He took a deep breath. "And before I go, I'm going to tell you about a few things I need you to do for me."

"Son…" I started to say but he waved his hand to silence me.

"No, I'm not wanting to be part of this journey you need to take. I get what you feel called to do, what you believe to be the right thing after all this time. But first, you can't head out tonight. There's a semi-decent hotel just down the street. Stay the night, sober up, and head out in the morning after you've had a good breakfast." He tapped one finger on the counter.

"Son, now don't go thinking you can tell me what to do. I…" The look on his face made me stop before saying more.

"This is non-negotiable. Either you agree, or I'll call the cops and have you arrested for drunk driving." He stood, walked over to the window, and snapped a picture of my car. Returning to stand beside me, he tapped a few times on the screen of the phone. "There, I've sent it to myself."

"Fine, what other demands do you have?" Wondering why he'd do such a thing.

He tapped two fingers on the counter, "Second, I'm a bit worried about you being on the road alone. However, I know you're never going to agree to anyone joining you. So, since you don't have your phone, I'm going to lend you mine. You can swing back by here on your way home." He gave my hand a quick squeeze, then wrote something down on a napkin. He put his cell on it, sliding both my way. "Here's the passcode and the phone number for that phone."

I watched as he continued to rap on the bar top, "You're not going to judge me? Try to convince me of how crazy I am?"

"No point in that, I think for once in your life you're doing what you should've been doing all along." He strode out of the room without looking back. "And, dude, while you're gone, I'm going to try to do the same." These words came reverberating back at me from the hallway as he disappeared into the gloom.

I tapped on the side of the computer for several moments, wondering how much to say to my wife or if it'd be best to be blunt. In the end, I opted for 'Don't worry, visiting a friend, be back in a week. Bruce'

But I knew she'd catch the lie in two seconds flat. In fifty-something years, I'd never left our little town in Colorado. I didn't have any friends who lived more than ten miles from our house. And she knew each and every one of them.

The lies had to stop, right this instant.

I stared back up at the rabbit on the wall. He still didn't have any answers for me; his glassy eyes remained blank. As much as I hated to admit it, that young buck Ryan was right. Nancy deserved a phone call. However, in my current state that wouldn't be possible. The drive to Texas wasn't exactly short. I'd kill some of the time trying to hash this out with my wife. Thus, she'd have to fuss and stew until tomorrow.

After deleting my first attempt at an email to Nancy, I sat for a moment in front of the blank screen watching the cursor blink. 'Call tomorrow with an explanation. Bruce.' KISS—keep it simple, stupid. And hit send before I changed my mind.

Staring at the computer once again, I took in a deep breath. Debating the words to send to this unknown entity I wanted more than anything to connect with. After several starts and stops, the message began to take shape.

Hi Jenny,

Thanks for contacting me.

I'm sure you're angry at me for abandoning you and your mother, and, well, for a lot of things. I'm sure that you've felt like I never cared about you, and I hate that you might have let those thoughts enter your mind even for a second. Because the truth is not a day has gone by where you haven't been in my thoughts, in my heart.

Never knowing you has been my biggest regret.

So, yes, I wish to meet you. To tell you what happened, why I couldn't be your father. But it has to be where this started, where I met your mother.

Can you meet me in Texas in a few days?

I know it's short notice but I'm headed out that way now. The best way to reach me is at this phone number.

Bruce

After putting Ryan's number into the message, I reviewed it several times. Taking a deep breath, my finger shook as I held it over the touchpad. The arrow icon wavering over the 'send' button on the screen. The blue of the button faded in and out as my vision blurred, my eyes squinting and my heart pounding out a loud rhythm.

Now or never.

Tapping on the pad, the message disappeared.

The end. Or the beginning.

I dropped a few bills on the counter, snatched up Ryan's phone, then shuffled out the door without waiting for him to come back into the room.

I was never good at goodbyes.

Acknowledgements

I have to say a big thank you to the staff at the U.S. Army Medical Museum at Fort Sam Houston in San Antonio, Texas. They were so gracious to me during my visit as I wandered around the museum and then examined various materials in their archives. Because of this time, the portion of this book surrounding Army Medics became much richer and more detailed. I'm forever in your debt.

About the Author

Leigh has spent the better part of the last thirty years involved in homeless and poverty advocacy in one way or another. Her first novel, *Road Home*, was born out of this work. She wanted to make people think about their lives and how they live, but most importantly, about how they treat others and how they want to be treated. The other novels in her *Broken Roads* Series are *Road to Freedom, Finding the Real Road,* and *The Road West*. These stories examine how our lives don't always follow the path we choose, yet somehow, we must pick up the broken pieces and move on.

Leigh's most recent novel is her most personal yet. *Lost Father* is a glimpse into the journey of one man as he deals with the aftermath of getting his girlfriend pregnant. The *Path to Family* Series will highlight the moving and hopeful story of adoption from the perspectives of those involved. Leigh is delighted to share her personal adoption experience with her readers.

Leigh has been interviewed on several podcasts and radio shows. She loves to inspire others to find their voice, explore the world, and never be left out of the conversation. Her passion lies in crafting inspiring novels that impact readers on a deep emotional level. Through her storytelling, she aims to inspire, uplift, and provoke thoughtful conversations. Even more fulfilling for Leigh is giving back to those in need. A portion of the proceeds from her novels goes directly to charities that serve those experiencing homelessness and poverty.

While Leigh may be relatively new to writing, she's not finished by far. Leigh loves to travel, paint, and hike. You never know where she'll end up next, for she's on her own journey of discovery.

www.ingramcontent.com/pod-product-compliance
Lightning Source LLC
Chambersburg PA
CBHW071401120626
46546CB00002B/770